How to Discover your Vocation

By Dana Dumitrascu

With Gratitude

I dedicate this book to my Spiritual Teacher, Master Choa Kok Sui, the Founder of Pranic Healing and Arhatic Yoga. It was the greatest blessing of my lifetime so far, to have found his teachings and to have learned from his most senior disciples. My gratitude will forever go to Master Marilag Mendoza, Master Stephen Co, Master Hector Ramos and Francesca Angrisano for being such dedicated and inspiring representatives of our Great Teacher. My deepest desire is to continue to learn and understand the teachings, with their help, for many years to come. May the wisdom imparted through Arhatic Yoga and Pranic Healing allow me to grow enough so that I understand how use my time wisely in my work and relationships, and how to be of better service.

I am grateful to my husband, Ioan, for believing in my work and for his constant support as I developed my method in the recent years and wrote this book. My own hopes for the impact of this book and of my vocational discovery method are first of all related to the lives of our six children: Sophie, Ana, Teo, Victor, George and Lia-Francesca. As I wrote this book, their ages ranged from 15 to 2. My biggest wish for them, aside from living a healthy and long life, and of being blessed with finding the right long-term partner, is that they find their vocation.

I want to thank my parents, Magda and Adrian, for being my first great teachers of life's three most important pillars: Love, Intelligence and Will.

Introduction

Seen from a socio-economic perspective, vocational discovery is a crucial part of the overall education and labor systems. It is directly connected to population rate of employment, employees' level of engagement and loyalty, and with productivity. But it is also connected to people's understanding they are a part of a larger social structure within which they contribute their most precious resources: their time and their abilities, through their work.

In my opinion, if every teenager would go through a vocational discovery process around the age of sixteen, there would be much less unemployment, less reasons for mid-life crises and divorces all around the world. I'll talk more about how vocation and personal life are connected later on in the book.

The discovery method that I created can be used by anyone from any educational system around the world. It also can be used at any age past the age of fourteen. Why fourteen? Because, as I learned from people much wiser than me, who mastered an understanding of the future of work, there should be a certain sequence of facilitating learning and instilling values when it comes to educating our young.

Primary education should go all the way to the age of fourteen, and should teach the child what his place is within his social group, emphasizing his group relations, which will lay the foundation for his adult relations.

It is in the second phase of education, ages fourteen to twenty one, where I would like my method to make the biggest difference. High schools and then colleges or trade schools should train teenagers for their future profession, which will become their *mode of life*. Every person who chooses a vocation enters a world that is both limiting and full of opportunities. It is limiting because it carves out a certain life path, making other life paths improbable. But the opportunities for fulfillment through one's work, if done with dedication and *in service*, are the reward of a vocational life.

The bigger purpose of this discovery method is to instill in people, and especially young people, the desire to belong to a more service-minded humankind. Individual gifts are to be recognized and developed, but only because they are gifts to be shared for the benefit of others, not for one's own satisfaction.

I wish that the two major ideas of this book do leave a mark on you, the reader. The first one is that the value of the individual self begins with finding his talents and abilities and that value turns to contribution when one finds their vocation. The second fact is that there is *only one humanity*, which must be served regardless of nationality, religion, skin color and other conditioning which limit the amplitude of the service and impact we can have on the lives of others.

This book presents introspective tools which you can easily understand with the mind. But wouldn't it be easier if a wiser part, or a higher part of ourselves (some of us call it soul) would somehow communicate, early on, what our purpose was? I sometimes think of a telling scene in the Disney cartoon, **Tinkerbell**. Tinkerbell, a fairy character, needs to work out her place in Pixie Hollow, where she was brought after she was born. During a wonderfully-depicted vocational discovery ritual, she learns that her talent is to be one of the tinkers. I wish I would have created such an integrated ritual where a person's personality and soul would simultaneously *know* which is the work one is here to do.

This method keeps away the directiveness of others, that is other people's desire of *telling* you what your vocation *should be* and perhaps **whom** your soulmate *should be*. My advice is that, *during your discovery process, it is better to keep away from techniques which claim that another person or the use of a certain substance can tell you the "truth" about any important aspect of your life*. I have had my own experiences with several directive techniques myself, which lay at the intersection of esotericism and pseudo-psychology, and I concluded that every true introspective method allows **you** to find the answers. You should not accept to be **told** what to do with your life. Guiding someone, especially your children, is not the same thing as telling them what to do.

But, for now, we are still in the phase where it does take some time to discover our path. For now, we are still caught in the paradigm of *making a living*. Because of this paradigm, when people start thinking about work, they make it a means towards a materially comfortable life, not a link to soul's realization. I often think of how educational methods could be changed in focus, from getting people to *make a living*, to teaching the mental and emotional qualities necessary to live a fulfilling and useful life.

I believe that the individualistic, *I only care about my own success* paradigm, is on its way out of the collective consciousness of our planet. Developing one's abilities doesn't make one selfish or individualistic. Thinking you are different, special, unique, is not wrong. Desiring to have success and be appreciated are not narcissistic traits. *But the individual exists as part of a group and for the benefit of the group*, and his or her success will always be measured by the overall success of the larger group where they live their day to day life.

A person who found their vocation is, in my opinion, more collaborative. That is also because, if one finds their vocation early on, they would have saved precious time which they will spend in service of their group, community, nation and, of course, humankind. Unless one finds their vocation early on, let's say, before the age of 28, one will keep spending their life trying to find other types of work, thinking that *the right one* will be the next one.

Also, those who found their vocation no longer feel the need to chase recognition in their career, to receive awards, to be nominated for this or for that. Instead, they attain the peace of mind needed to focus on service.

People search for many things hoping for tools or strategies that can quickly solve their personal relationship, their relationship with their children, their finances, and their health. We turn to personal development, to spirituality, when we go through times of uncertainty, through a life crisis or even deal with depression or despair: one may lose a parent, go through a rough divorce, or lose their job. Worse things, such as having to escape life threatening circumstances in your city or home country can change almost all aspects of your life. External circumstances at times may be crippling and even the strongest person needs help to find balance and hope again.

This book may be about discovering your vocation, but once you have clarity about the work you're meant to do, you will come to enjoy a higher and more constant level of inner balance. Provided you have your health, your work is the one aspect of your life you can continue to enjoy, grow and share despite any other circumstance.

I am aware you may be here because you might have lost your job and needed to clarify your thoughts, needs and expectations before starting another job search. Or, perhaps, you're in college but you're unsure what to do next. Maybe you're the parent of a small child and you feel torn about going back to work at your previous job. You don't know if it's safe or smart to risk financial stability if you choose to work less or work more flexible hours in order to spend more time with your baby. Or you're in high school and need to clarify your choice of college or trade school. Perhaps your case is one of lack of motivation. You have no problem getting a job but a few weeks or months in, you lose your drive and enthusiasm and end up quitting after a short time.

In the journey of discovering the right path for our professional lives, we often encounter crossroads where the choices we make not only impact our careers but also ripple into the very fabric of our relationships, health, and overall well-being. It's a conundrum faced by many, from seasoned professionals contemplating entrepreneurship to aspiring artists navigating unsupportive environments.

For the experienced professional considering entrepreneurship, the fear of change and the weight of family responsibilities can loom large. Yet, fear is often a signal that we are on the cusp of growth, and that with the right mindset and strategies, we can navigate the transition successfully, while strengthening our relationships. By aligning our entrepreneurial pursuits with our values and priorities, we can create a business that not only sustains us financially but also enriches our personal lives.

Meanwhile, the aspiring artist grappling with an unsupportive environment may feel torn between passion and practicality.

Ultimately, the journey of self-discovery outlined in this book offers a roadmap for those who find themselves at a crossroads, uncertain of which path to take.

If you were to ask me today, what is the key ingredient for feeling fulfilled in life, I would honestly say it is discovering and practicing your vocation. Not only does it impact one's sense of meaning, but also one's longevity, and the success of your most meaningful personal relationships, with your life partner and children.

I have been guiding people through a process of choosing their vocation for the past half decade. It may not seem such a long time, and that is because the vocational discovery method I created started as coaching and counseling many more years ago. During the past five years I worked with hundreds of teenagers and adults. The former were mostly looking to decide which major to pick in college, while the latter came to me for various reasons – wishing to change professions or desiring to quit the corporate world, trying to find a more flexible job that would allow mothers of young children to spend more time at home. Some of the adults I met changed more than two careers in the last two years alone.

During the pandemic, so many people I worked with needed to find a new profession, start on a different work path because there was no longer need for what they had been doing, sometimes for many, many years.

But while uncertainty and the unknown are seeds for creativity, one thing kept on raising my concern but also enticed my curiosity when it came to the people I served: why are there so few people who just **know**, are **certain** of their choice of vocation?

Why so much confusion among the majority of the population? In my counseling, I had mostly worked with people in Romania, but my own life experience was diverse enough that work-related fears, lack of commitment to a certain path, lack of trust in one's potential and abilities, was something I had seen and worked with in the United States as well, where I lived for a whole decade of my life before returning to my native Romania in 2018.

In the bustling streets of New York City, amidst the whirlwind of emotions that accompany divorce mediation, a practice I trained in staring 2016, I found myself pondering a profound question: could one's vocation be a significant factor in couples' wellbeing? This question led me to explore the insights of renowned relationship expert John Gottman, whose research sheds light on the dynamics of successful partnerships.

It became apparent that the notion of compatibility extended far beyond surface-level differences, such as divergent career paths. Rather, it delved into the deeper realms of personal fulfillment, resilience, and emotional strength. Couples where one or both partners were perpetually discontent with their work or frequently changed jobs seemed to face heightened challenges in their relationships. This phenomenon transcended mere financial concerns; it spoke to the essence of personal power, intelligence, and the ability to navigate adversity with confidence and perseverance.

Gottman's wisdom on couple compatibility resonated deeply as I observed how partners in thriving relationships often shared a mutual admiration and respect for each other's professional accomplishments. When individuals found fulfillment and meaning in their work, they emanated a positive energy that reverberated throughout their relationship. Conversely, those who harbored dissatisfaction or resentment towards their jobs risked burdening their partners with a constant stream of negativity, draining the relationship of its vitality.

In essence, the correlation between vocational satisfaction and relationship fulfillment became increasingly evident. A partner who thrived professionally brought a sense of purpose and fulfillment to the relationship, enriching it with positive energy and mutual respect. Discontentment in one's career could cast a shadow over the partnership, placing undue strain on the relationship as it became the sole source of positivity amidst a sea of dissatisfaction. There is a clear and direct connection between Work and Love.

No other author I ever read said it more concisely and more profoundly than Lebanese-American poet, Kahlil Gibran, so I will infuse these pages with the energy of his wisdom:

"Work is love made visible. And if you cannot work with love but only with distaste, it is better that you should leave your work and sit at the gate of the temple and take alms of those who work with joy. For if you bake bread with indifference, you bake a bitter bread that feeds but half man's hunger. And if you grudge the crushing of the grapes, your grudge distils a poison in the wine."

Gibran's eloquent words captured the profound connection between work and love, highlighting the importance of infusing our tasks with genuine passion and devotion. Beyond mere productivity, wholehearted engagement with our work is essential for psychological balance and fulfillment.

***

I entered the world of therapists and counselors in 2016, after seventeen years of working in communications; first, as a news anchor and talk-show host, and then as a leadership and public speaking trainer and communications specialist. I was always very curious about people's stories. Biographies have been my favorite books to read, and ever since I can remember, I preferred heroes with superpowers, such as the Gods and Demi-Gods of Greek mythology or fantastic characters with a great mind, like Sherlok Holmes or a great spirit, like Dorothy in the Wizard of Oz. I liked it most when people overcame obstacles and realized their dreams.

My own journey to finding my vocation was long, and I said "this must be it" several times. Luck and opportunity put me in a first job as a news anchor at the young age of nineteen. I was "certain" I found my vocation, especially because I had been dreaming of becoming a journalist since I was twelve years old. I spent two years in television in Bucharest, Romania, and, as much as I felt being in front of the camera came so naturally to me, I don't regret leaving that environment. I didn't know then that as a news anchor, I was able to use many of my natural abilities, but what didn't fit with me on a long run was the News Department lifestyle. That lifestyle did not fit my physical body, or my emotional body. These are concepts you will learn about in this book.

The pressure of going out there, finding and putting together all sorts of alarming or downright catastrophic pieces of news, always being on the go without time for anything else in my personal life was not the right lifestyle for me. Emotionally, the high level of judgment, envy and constant gossip that used to go around News offices, especially directed to female News anchors, was not something I was able to deal with long-term. I loved being in front of the camera and I was a very good news anchor. But that didn't ultimately mean my vocation was to be a news journalist for decades, living my daily life in that pace and managing huge pressure to produce daily results.

However, speaking in public and in front of the camera are definitely two of my most important natural abilities and I was given the opportunity to grow and test these talents in real-life situations rather than just in my imagination.

This may be your case, too. You might have had a job or two where some things fit. You liked parts of your job but disliked others. You're a creative person who chose to work in marketing for a consulting firm and you liked the intellectual challenges of the job. After a while, you found that there is not enough space for you to manifest your creativity as often as you liked and no need for your creative writing. You may begin to label your work as a smart compromise. You get good pay and also do a job you don't totally hate. Let's say, if I were to ask you, that you like about 60% of the things you do at your workplace on a day to day basis. Like so many people, you try to make up for the other aspects of yourself, some of which we call talents or abilities or interests, on vacation or during the weekend.

How many consultants paint in their free time? Do you try to express your natural talents and abilities mostly in your free time, but always feel time is too short to grow that part of yourself you feel makes you special, makes you joyful?

You may be inclined to say: *what is so terrible if I have a good job with good pay and I only like it 60% of the time? Or I can only express 60% of my abilities through my work? That is a pretty good life to have and perhaps I should just be grateful I can afford a comfortable life for me and my loved ones.*

These arguments hold their weight most of the time, but there comes a moment in life when you will not be able to compensate for the lack of fulfillment with the material benefits of your job. Isn't it obvious that there are people, even people you know, who have found their vocation, are doing it every day, receive good pay for it, are fulfilled and happy? Perhaps that professor you had in college, or that mechanic who always fixes your car, or your child's nursery teacher, or even your nail specialist or hair stylist. They do their work day after day and completely love it. You can see and feel that they are totally meant to do it. Not 60% of the time, but all of the time.

Far from me the intention of this being a philosophy book. This is a practical book at the end of which you will have created a framework, an individual framework of what makes a profession right for you.

But I feel I need to say this, even though it may sound dramatic. We fail to understand that out of a lifespan of 80 years, we spend a little less than 1/3 of our lifetime working. By comparison, we also spend 1/3 of our entire lifetime sleeping. That leaves 1/3 of our lifetime free to experience childhood, the teen years, retirement, and some free time we manage to squeeze in after we get a job. That may sound terrible and plainly depressing when you realize that if you are in a relationship that's bad for you and also in a job you dislike, and you are over the age of twenty five, that pretty much sums up all your time other than sleep.

Have you asked yourself how would it feel to go to work happy and enthusiastic, feeling your contribution makes a difference in people's lives and at the end of the day you know your worth, you are being useful and authentic?

How important is it to get the vocational part right early in your adult life? Ideally, before you marry and have children, before you choose your partner.

I say: first, fall in love with your vocation, and through it, you'll love yourself. You will look at the world differently afterwards. As the Universe supports that which we do with clarity, being on a clear path will bring along the right companion who will love and admire your vocational self, too.

Before we dive into the vocational discovery method, I will talk a little bit about the importance of making independent choices about the big things in your life. Otherwise, what is the point of you discovering your vocational framework and then just overlooking it when you apply for a new job that your friend or parent recommended?

External factors which impact your decisions in a major way, keeping you in a job or a relationship where you're unsure you want to be, are mental and emotional pressure points that will ultimately constrain you to express your personal truth outside of either that job or relationship. And most likely, in the absence of those pressure points, you would make different life choices.

Imagine this case, which happened several times in my practice: the parents of a teenager sent him to me because he or she seems confused about which college to apply to. The parents are, let's say, a doctor and a financial consultant, or a math teacher and an engineer, or a psychologist and a business owner. But the son, who is seventeen, wants to become a chef and this is something new that surfaced as the decision about college approached, although they admit that their son was making them breakfast every weekend ever since he was seven years old and always baked all the cakes and pastries for birthdays and parties. Now the parents are scared. Scared of the unknown. For nothing in their past and professional reality can tell them how the life of a chef might unfold. For what they know, it can be financially risky. So in many cases and in many cultures, parents have the biggest impact over the child's career option or short list of careers. Fine, they say: if you don't want to be a doctor, be a dentist. Or be an IT specialist, a programmer, that's super safe for the future.

Almost all the options parents guide, push or, emotionally and mentally influence their children into going for, after high-school, have a pretty clear and predictable path, both economically and socially. They make *sense. So what could be wrong about that?*

We would not be mistaken to conclude that in our society, almost everyone embarking on the adventure called adult life has had a *pre-determined choice of career* made for him or her by either the parents or the immediate circle of influencers, like relatives and teachers.

Most parents in today's society guide their children towards *practical careers.* Of course, you want and **you need** your work to be practical. Your work is love, it is infused with love, but work must be a practical thing. It must provide financial sustenance and allow you to continue to grow your skills and expertise and be of real service to other people. Just sitting on a pillow meditating all day may sound spiritual, but we must make sure we have a useful, practical vocation, that serves other people's needs.

The mechanism of making the choice of vocation, of allowing a new possibility to emerge for you, is important in the process of *living life on your terms. For that, you should be taught how to* make your own decisions.

We make only a few really important choices during our life as creators of our lives, which, in turn, determine the quality of our life and relationships, and it would be really amazing if we would be able to make them from a place of possibility and not fear or complacency.

Fear-based decisions usually indicate the person gave into the influence of many external sources such as members of their family (who know what's best for him or her) to people in their school, community, workplace, or among their closest friends.

I think about the plague of confusion our teenagers go though regarding their own path. You might say, well, it's natural not to know which way to go when you're fourteen. That's why you have family and professors to guide you. This can be helpful up to a point, but think about it for a second. This system of taking children through the school system and then having family and educators **point them** in different directions which ultimately lead to them deciding which profession to pick, is the very system that leaves so many people unemployed all over the world even though they are college graduates. This system may be the biggest culprit in what we call mid-life crisis, the point when so many people wonder if this is the life they are supposed to live, if they are supposed to be this frustrated with different aspects of their work. **Should the work you do be the choice of others?**

Many U.S. surveys try to capture the levels of people's satisfaction with their work. A factor I like to look at is the level of employee engagement worldwide. This factor points to the length of time an employee will stay in an organization. Lately, it has become harder and harder for organizations across the globe to retain employees long term. They may be satisfied with aspects of their work, such as their level of pay, or level of responsibilities and self-governance, or their work-life balance, but, still, companies are unable to retain them long term. **I asked myself, why?**

I think the answer has to do with the distinction between job and vocation. An important distinction is the life-long commitment one has towards one's vocation, the high level of enthusiasm for doing that work every day which does not significantly decrease after a couple of years, and the constant desire to acquire more expertise in that area. In other words, the desire to be better, to serve others better.

In this book, the journey of vocational discovery will be revealed through the stories of ten people. The stories emerged from a mixture of personal narratives of people I worked with, and stories of other people whose lives inspired me. In each of them, I tried to offer what I call "actionable wisdom" for you to consider and use in your own discovery process. The usual vocational discovery process I guide people through, in the one-to-one setup, lasts five sessions. Each session reveals one or two concepts and key tools of vocational discovery and, as people go through them, they get closer and closer to understanding their vocational framework. In the book, each of the ten people whose stories will help you reflect on your own process, happens at a certain moment during their discovery process, bringing forth the introspective power of each discovery tool and each important distinction. If you follow each story and go through the same exercises as the characters do, you will end up with your own vocational framework at the end. I can't guide you in person through deeper moments, such as visualizations, but you will get a sense how the discovery process unfolds, through each character's journey.

Some of you have been searching for their vocation for several years already, and I am here to try to guide your search for the *right* answer.

And since you're just about to dive into these stories, I need to begin by telling you that the search will be useless and potentially filled with several *fake career matches* for as long as **you think of your work as something that is meant to fulfill you, to give you pleasure, significance, success.**

Usually, when adults who have already been employed for at least three-to-five years come to see me, they begin complaining along these same lines:

I really don't want to do this kind of work anymore…

What do you want to do? I invariably ask.

I want to travel, read, paint, sing, hike, see my friends more, be with my family, do things **I love!**

I know, at that point, that the person sitting in front of me hasn't yet been exposed to the lives of vocational people who do a lot of service for others. Instead, they grew up in an individualistic culture that professes one's comfort and happiness as the ultimate goal of life.

Your work is the tool through which your individual existence becomes integrated with the larger purpose of a group and has an impact within that group or a larger community.

The right vocation, thus, integrates your whole life, instead of creating a separate reality just for you. The right vocation, put to the service of a group or larger community, should never compromise your peace of mind or those personal relationships you care about deeply and are right for you.

Throughout my own story, as long as I kept searching for the next thing to *define* all of me or *reward* me for what I was doing, I was easily distracted from each of the several professions that made up the first seventeen years of my career. I felt I was *entitled* to that, *entitled* to this, better suited for this career or for that.

As soon as I came across the path of service I recognized its truth. It happened two-fold: in the same year, 2016, I met my mediation mentor, Kenneth Neumann, and entered the practical and spiritual world of Pranic Healing, meeting two of the eight Pranic Healing teachers: Masters Marilag and Glenn Mendoza from New Jersey. Only then, by observing the life and work of these three people, I began to understand that life *feels* empty and frustrating unless we live it in service of others.

Chapter 1 - Elise and the Concept of Direct Utility

You must have asked yourself, what is the difference between a job and a vocation? Perhaps you wonder if you have a vocation at all. Have you hopped from one job to another in the recent years and this left you disillusioned and anxious about ever finding the right work for you? This was the case of Elise, when she came to see me, about eighteen months ago.

At thirty two, Elise found herself caught in a cycle of job hopping, restlessly searching for a place where she could anchor her thoughts and talents. It was in the midst of this turbulent journey that she heard about my work, and hoped that my guidance would bring her some clarity.

Elise was a slim, hyperactive figure with an eager gleam in her eye. When she arrived in my office, clutched in her arms was a tiny baby poodle, a fluffy bundle that balanced her restless spirit. I couldn't help but notice how Elise's demeanor seemed to oscillate between childlike enthusiasm and a deep-seated yearning for something that was still to be discovered.

As the first session unfolded, her story began to unravel. She had been an event organizer, a coffee equipment sales woman, an Audio Book Library development and sales manager, a manager for a Food Delivery Company, and all these just in the past year.

It took about two sessions talking about her most recent disappointments with employers who didn't understand her real value, for her to tell me about her love for the violin, a passion that had been abruptly silenced by her mother's desire for practicality. Elise had been playing the violin for almost a decade in her childhood and teen years. Her mother's weight of expectations had led Elise down a path of conformity, culminating in a series of unfulfilling jobs that left her feeling adrift and disconnected.

Elise's story doesn't yet have a happy ending that I know of. Eventually, during our final two sessions, a glimmer of hope appeared on the horizon as she secured two promising job interviews that matched her interests and abilities. Excitement filled the air of our last session as she weighed her options, ultimately choosing a position that seemed to promise stability and purpose. I hoped this job would be long-lasting, but it wasn't. Elise's newfound sense of direction was short-lived, too. Three weeks after starting with her new employer, a sense of disillusionment crept in as she realized that her new manager, too, failed to recognize her true talents and potential.

In a heartfelt message to me, she expressed a deep-seated need to feel useful and important, a yearning that echoed the unspoken desires of her heart.

I chose Elise's story to show you the main difference between getting a job and finding your vocation. This book, just like my work, does not prepare you for a job interview. It is a method of clarification of where it is most likely for you to be happy, useful and fulfilled while using your abilities to the most.

If you do a little research, you'll see that the word vocation is defined like this: "a person's employment or main occupation, especially regarded as worthy and requiring dedication."

Vocational work used to describe mostly technical types of work which needed practical and technical skills that high school graduates opted for instead of going to college.

Traditional vocations included being a firefighter, a shoemaker, a carpenter, an electrician, a baker, a nurse, a plumber. To specialize in such work required one to go to trade school and obtain a certification, while spending significant time as an apprentice before starting to practice. My own maternal grandfather was an exquisite tailor in Romania, and he was sent by his mother to work as an apprentice for a tailor in Bucharest, at the age of 11. His apprenticeship lasted more than 7 years and he practiced his trade for over 65 years. He was a great mentor to many apprentice tailors.

A vocation is also defined as "a strong feeling of suitability for a particular career or occupation."

This book, of which each chapter presents another discovery tool, will teach you how to test if a particular career or occupation is suitable for you.

There's another thing we should clarify right from the beginning. Can a person have multiple vocations or is a vocation a lifetime commitment, like it was for my grandfather?

Is it possible to be a fully capable, super talented tailor, work on this vocation for 20 years and then feel that you have had enough of it? It is possible to reach a state of plateau where you feel you cannot go any higher in terms of your expertise, but you can always go higher in number of people you serve or level of innovation or teaching in your field.

A vocational circle is complete, in my opinion, when, after having become an expert in what you do, which could take at least a decade, you teach it or you help take the area to a next level. If you stop before you get to the teaching part, it is very likely that the lifestyle of that profession doesn't suit you anymore. You'll learn, further in the course, that a beneficial lifestyle is one that suits you *physically, mentally and emotionally*. Let's say you have been a successful tailor for 20 years. You have also done some teaching but you feel you can't do this anymore. Perhaps the profession has become too demanding on your physical body. Perhaps your legs and your arms, which you've counted on every day to help you serve, are tired and you can't sustain sitting at the sewing machine or stand at the tailoring table for over ten hours a day any more. What can you do? You could teach more, take in more apprentices. You could integrate more of mentoring and innovating in your profession. You don't have to quit it because you feel too old or too tired to sustain the physical aspect of it.

On the other hand, it *is* possible to have two or even three vocations throughout one's life. One can be a lawyer for twenty years and a sound engineer for the next fifteen. However, when such things happen, you will find that the vocation which took over later in life had always been a passion earlier in life. Sometimes, it means it could have been the ONLY vocation, the only type of work that a person could have done had he or she better introspected before choosing their first profession. Sometimes, people choose to spend twenty years in a profession that served for the development of one's mental abilities, while the second one will serve to develop one's emotional abilities. Usually, the second vocation is more service-oriented.

The *perfect* vocation develops a person mentally and emotionally in a balanced way. That is one of the key indicators one has found the vocational "home".

In the book, I will use several words to talk about work: I will use the word **job** to refer to what people generally call their 9-to-5 employment for which they receive a fixed salary each month. This is the majority of the world's population. I will use the word **vocation** to describe what I call the soul's way of best serving on earth through work. I will sometimes use the word **profession** to describe the specific skills assigned to a trade in which one becomes an expert. You cannot be a *professional* if you are not specialized in a set of skills and in a field of work. Two years in a job, plus two in another do not make you a professional nor is it possible for you to say that you had two *professions* already.

Never before has any other generation questioned so much the human and emotional value of the time they spend working. People didn't use to think whether their job is good for their mental health. Today, the overwhelming culturescope of mental health made all of us aware that *relationships and jobs can be toxic*. We talk about people's behaviors being toxic, and that can also apply to job-related stress.

Burn out and depression are two severe side effects of people being physically and emotionally exhausted working at a job that carries at least one stressful aspect which impacts the quality of their life.

Humanity's evolution has already awakened in the young generation a sort of scanner for authenticity. In the past, you could pull off going to a job you hated for years and years just to make ends meet and pay the bills. This is no longer possible in the age we're in. The level and vibration of consciousness has shifted and the young generation talks a lot about purpose, freedom. In the future of work, Artificial Intelligence will push us to the corner and squeeze every ounce of creativity out of us. Before becoming "Homo Deus[1]", we must allow our society to free our young ones' minds from many old beliefs and behaviors related to work, so that, instead of dreading it, the young generation becomes aware of their journey as creators through their work. I don't mean it in the sense of creating art, but in the sense of being able to live our relationships and our profession with the mindset of a creator rather than a skilled laborer executing tasks and using tools. *Much of the automated part will be done for us and what will stay will be creative expression and emotional connection.*

The more useful one's work will be to the mental, emotional and physical wellbeing of people around them, the more crisis-proof it will be. And talking about crisis, how can you make sure that the vocation you choose is crisis-proof? A big crisis, such as the Covid-19 pandemic, led me to discover a concept I called **Direct Utility**.

It was when I told the following story to Elise that she, in turn, told me about her past as a violin player.

It was in the summer of 2020 and I was teaching and counseling people online. I was working on Zoom, like so many other people around the world. If anything, my work intensified in 2020, also because so many people were now unsure of the future of their job.

I remember that it was during a Sociology Class I was teaching students that I found myself explaining what became the concept of direct utility. I used the example of a friend of mine who is a shoe-maker to explain it and it became a part of the distinctions I make when I start guiding people in the vocational discovery process.

---

[1] Reference to the term coined by Professor Yuval Noah Harari in his book, Homo Deus.

Another big difference between finding your vocation and "holding on to a job", no matter how "good" it is in terms of giving you financial comfort, is that a vocation is more likely to be *crisis-proof*.

The first distinction I make when telling this story to my clients is that one's work is 100% **useful** to the end client, to the beneficiary of the work when there is no need for an intermediary between the provider and the receiver.

Serving a client directly, without intermediaries, is a characteristic of vocational work or labor. In the example I'm about to give, the pandemic also hit the business of a luxury shoe maker in Bucharest. Before the pandemic, M the shoemaker was making about 8-10 pairs of bespoke leather shoes and selling them for a high price of between 1000 and 3000 Euro/pair. Foreigners living in Bucharest and wealthy businessmen would be the main clients to afford these high quality shoes. Before the pandemic, M the shoemaker employed four other people: he had an assistant shoe maker, a secretary/receptionist, a part-time social media specialist and a courier running errands.

When you look at a person's level of direct utility you look to measure it in relation to his or her work for the end client directly. So, M's clients buy shoes and M is a shoe maker. **He obviously has a 100% degree of direct utility to his clients**. His assistant shoemaker also makes shoes so he also directly serves the clients with the end product they buy. However, he does not have all the expertise M has, which is to make luxury leather shoes. The assistant shoe maker provides a more rudimentary service. Though a shoe maker himself, without M's designs and expertise, the assistant shoemaker would be unable to 100% serve the client at the requested level of expertise. But let's say that the assistant shoe maker does have a 70 to 80% level of direct utility to the clients.

Moving on to the secretary, we can start imagining that the degree of direct utility to the client is already much lower than the one of the assistant shoe maker. A receptionist does not make the end product. She is an intermediary of a higher degree because she does create a connection with the clients and has an important role in keeping the clients loyal, by pampering them with chocolates and champagne when they are in the shop, sending them Holiday gifts and keeping M informed about important changes in the clients' schedule or even color and fabric preferences. But regardless of how precious a secretary's help might be in keeping the clients loyal and happy with M's brand, her percentage of direct utility is not higher than 40%. When you start looking at low direct utility percentages, what this tells you is that that particular position, that job, is replaceable and that the client would not be terribly affected by the change.

The degree of direct utility is even lower for the social media specialist and the courier who delivers the shoes to clients. If M chooses to replace them, the client, the buyer of his shoes, would be so little affected that it wouldn't really make a difference.

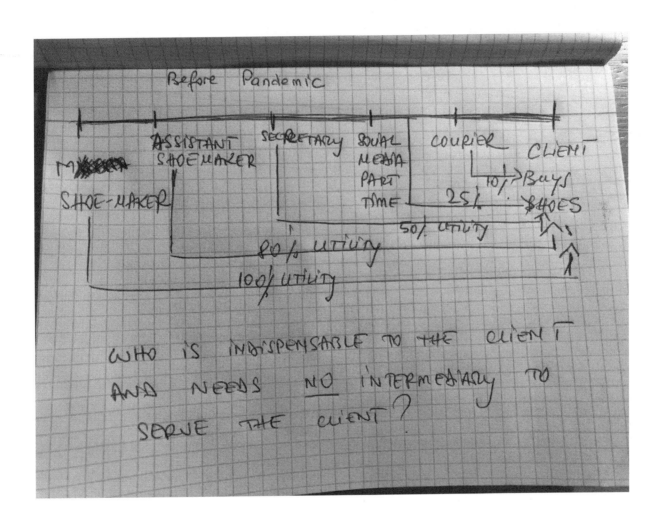

So, let's just say this: for your profession to matter and your expertise to be crisis-proof, your level of direct utility to the end client has to be over 70%. Anything under, and in any crisis of any sort, you will be considered an intermediary of the work, service or product given to the client, and thus replaceable.

In M's case, once the pandemic hit and he had no more orders, he fired everyone within the course of three months and then, around the end of summer in 2020, when he started to receive an occasional order, he served those clients completely by himself for a while.

Even if you're right now looking for a job, ask yourself, what is it that the client is buying from that company/organization? And are you a direct provider or the specialist (even a junior one) working on exactly that product or service?

Let's take another example, one I can extract as a life lesson from my own professional life.

I already told you about my very first job as a news anchor. Working in the news department of a TV station as a news anchor, delivering the news to the audience (who was the end-client) made me have a super high level of direct utility. To me that meant that I was an essential employee there, which made me harder to fire (if I did a good job). However, having the same abilities as before, and even more experience, I left the TV world and worked as a marketing officer in an international law firm for three years. I did that so that I could make more money, work in an international environment and be able to finish college. Life in a news office leaves very little time for anything else. However, the moment I got that job, I became an intermediary with a very low level of direct utility to the firm's end client. Lawyers were the ones directly serving the clients, which made me easily replaceable and my work not essential. Human nature has a calling, a desire to feel highly useful. No wonder so many women who had not found their vocation prior to becoming mothers do not want to resume working in a multinational firm on an intermediary position, once they had a baby. At home, they are 100% directly useful to the baby and they know that when they go back to work their position will fulfill that need in a very little degree.

So be mindful when you choose the place you work in. It is very different to be an HR officer in an accounting firm or law firm than it is to be an HR specialist in a recruiting firm. The latter case makes you the specialist, serving the client with abilities that are directly useful to him. The former makes you an intermediary, meaning that some of the key work done by accountants or lawyers for clients needs some side service from you, one that is not essential none the less.

The only time I felt 100% useful was when I was playing the violin, said Elise, while caressing Mina the poodle, her eyes watery. *I didn't have any doubts that what I was doing was good, and I could see how much people enjoyed it. The hours and hours I spent practicing every day were worth it. But my parents divorced when I was 15 and my mom, being the* **general** *she is, decided I must embrace a practical profession that can ensure financial stability. So I studied business* *management and even did a Masters in Hotel Management. It is too late to go back to playing the violin.*

Ever since she left the world of music to immerse in a different one that, as far as we explored during the vocational process, did not mirror her main natural abilities, Elise lost her compass. Nothing seemed to *match* who she felt she was and she also didn't feel *important, significant enough* in the jobs she was doing. Though many of them were intellectually stimulating, and she liked the intellectual challenge, none put her in the position of **high direct utility to the *end receiver of the work*** which she experienced as a violin player. *Vocational people feel the urge of being useful in a way that leaves no space between their work and their client.* A hairdresser may feel much more useful and inclined to stay in her profession for over a decade than a corporate manager who has a *significant* title and a larger paycheck but can never reach the end client because of the internal hierarchies which de-personalize work and make it an expression of a company's mission rather than of the individual's calling to serve someone else directly.

Can everyone have a 100% level of direct utility to clients? Isn't the capitalist world based on an intricate puzzle where large organizations need hundreds of jobs and positions to keep going, to grow, to serve larger markets? All I am saying is that in any crisis or big change, be it a pandemic or an economic crisis, the first jobs being cut are the ones with low direct utility to the clients.

Before you finish this Chapter, I want you to think about the times in your life, personal or professional, when you served other people directly through something you know or something you did. If you feel like writing them down, do so and write as many things as you can, even the times when you made lemonade and sold it at the lemonade stand to thirsty neighbors on a hot summer day. Cooking and then feeding the homeless at a homeless shelter, leading a Boy Scout troop on a mountain trip and teaching survival skills, teaching a friend how to play the guitar even if you're not a master yet yourself.

The point is that you learn this new way of looking at the things you do, from the perspective of direct utility. This is important because a high degree of fulfillment and meaning are derived from directly serving someone.

Chapter 2 – Damian and the *The Five Guests at Dinner*

When Damian first came to me, I had been briefed thoroughly by his girlfriend and I was already expecting a young Jimmy Fallon to come into my office. Damian, unlike Elise, was a client I successfully guided during his decision-making and discovery process, with a clear result of our work together. This is why I prefer working with teenagers rather than adults: they don't have to un-think, un-believe and un-learn too many things about who they are and what their abilities are. *They are still closer to their natural calling.*

Damian sat down and looked around. It was past noon but he immediately asked if he could smoke in the balcony before the session began. He was barely eighteen, but I could tell he didn't just start smoking. I allowed him and I even offered him a cappuccino. He was *cool* and definitely wanted to look older than his years. In my counseling, I try my best to do two things: not judge, and not be directive, that is, not telling people what I think they should do.

His girlfriend was a year older than him and worked with me before becoming an Arts student. She gave me important details about Damian's situation. His parents didn't know he was coming to see me to discuss his post-high-school path, because they were certain it had been decided. *If you'd see his room ever since he was, like, seven, you could tell that he's all about the Radio. When we met, three years ago, I was already editor-in-chief of the high school's newspaper and radio station. He wanted my job right away; he wanted to be the Radio anchor. His voice is so captivating that the principal asked him to broadcast the high school weekly news in her place. During the past two years he was* **the voice** *presenting tens of high school events around town and even in other cities. And, last summer, he finally made it as an intern to this popular radio station, where he anchored a morning teen show for a month. After that, it's like he caught a bug. In our friends' circle, we call him Radio Boy.*

The problem is that his parents had made plans to move to Germany years ago, where their eldest daughter is finishing a Master's in medical engineering. It had been planned that Damian would apply to a college at the same University, an applied science school. Basically they mapped out his future since he was a junior in high school. They don't know that he was offered another summer job at the same Radio station for two months this summer. He doesn't have the guts to tell them he wants to stay in Romania and be **the Radio guy.**

Working with Damian got me looking more into the work of American psychologist, Anne Roe, who made significant contributions to our understanding of parental influence on their children's choice of profession. Her groundbreaking research shed light on the intricate dynamics that shape vocational development.

Roe claimed that parents play a crucial role in shaping their children's career aspirations through a combination of genetic, social, and environmental factors. She identified three main ways in which parents influence their children's career choices:

Parental Expectations: Roe found that parents often project their own aspirations onto their children, guiding them towards careers that align with their own values and interests. This can manifest in explicit expectations or subtle messages conveyed through familial dynamics, even small chit-chat at the dinner table.

Parental Behavior: Roe observed that children often model their career choices after their parents' behaviors and experiences. Whether through direct observation or subconscious emulation, children internalize their parents' attitudes towards work and success.

Parental Relationships: Roe emphasized the role of parent-child relationships in shaping vocational development. Positive, supportive relationships can foster confidence and autonomy in career decision-making, while strained or conflicted relationships may hinder exploration and self-discovery.

In her seminal work, Roe highlighted the profound impact of parental influence on children's vocational choices, stating:

"Parents who have professional or skilled jobs are likely to have children who aspire to the same. The home is the primary socializing agent, and parental roles and attitudes are crucial determinants of career development."

Furthermore, she noted:

"Children tend to choose a vocation that compensates for the things they perceive as lacking in their parents' careers. For example, a child of a workaholic parent may pursue a career that prioritizes work-life balance."

Roe's findings underscore the complex interplay between parental influence and individual agency in shaping vocational trajectories. While parents undoubtedly exert a significant influence,

Roe's work emphasizes the importance of fostering autonomy and self-awareness in children's career decision-making processes.

So, as the end of high school approached, Damian stood at a crossroads. He *knew* that, first of all, he was *feeling* that leaving his native country, his friends, his radio world, was not what he was meant to do. He loved and admired his parents so much, for how they raised him and his sister. Both his parents and his sister were *numbers* people. He told me that his abilities in communication, his passion for the radio must have been passed down by his uncle, his father's brother, who was a sports anchor and journalist.

His parents, on one hand, couldn't imagine leaving him behind and moving to Germany. They were also frowning upon the uncle's bachelor lifestyle which seemed never-ending. They had provided a great life for Damian and his sister. By the age of 18, Damian was used to what I call *the good life*. Without saying it in words, they were *showing* Damian that a *good life* needs a lot of money to sustain it, and a more practical career was more likely to keep him in the world he became accustomed with. The nice clothes, the vacations, the outings with friends at sporting events and concerts…things that can easily become chains around our dreams when we don't *know* that the things we enjoy turn into our prison unless they come hand in hand with the freedom to do what we love and love whom we like.

In the pages to follow, you, too, will bear witness to *The Five Guests at Dinner*, the introspective tool that got Damian to a point of clarity about his choice. Alongside with him, do the exercise for yourself.

Damian, I said, looking him in the eye, *your trip begins with an exercise I created about 4 years ago. Hundreds of people went through it, had fun doing it and learned one of the most important distinctions in my method of discovery. You will need your notebook and pen or pencil to write down every single little discovery you make, because there will be several in this session.*

This exercise is called the Five Guests at Dinner. Simply follow my guidance through it.

I want you to imagine that I am a good fairy. With my special powers, I create a parallel world for you, in which, starting tonight and for the next 365 evenings, you will be having dinner with five special guests. You can choose your setting, and, in fact, I want you to close your eyes for just a moment and imagine the perfect and most relaxing place where you would host a very special dinner with these five guests for the next 365 evenings, between 7 and 9 pm. The five guests will not change; they stay the same throughout the year, so you will get to know them really well. Close your eyes, take a deep breath, exhale, and imagine: where would you like to host this dinner? On the beach, hearing the waves crushing on the shore on a warm summer evening? In a beautiful rose garden? By a swimming pool? Take a moment to just imagine the setting for this dinner. Keep your eyes closed and relax. When you're ready and have decided on the perfect location to host this year-long dinner, write down the location you chose.

I gave him a little less than a minute. While he still had his eyes closed, I asked which location he chose. He said: *a movie set, I'd go for something classic, like a dinner table on the cruise ship in Some Like it Hot.*

I continued:

Now that you chose your dinner location, you will choose the five very special guests you'll be hosting. Again, the same five guests will be with you each evening during the next year. They can't be just anyone you think of. In fact, there are some rules about whom they can or cannot be. They **cannot be** *anyone you ever knew personally, not even for ten seconds, not even online. No one from your life, personal or professional. Who can they be, then?*

Characters you like, in fact characters you loved from Netflix, HBO or television series, movies, books or plays.

You know, those characters whose life fascinated you and you couldn't wait to watch another episode or read more of that book.

For me, one character that constantly inspired me in a movie was Audrey Hepburn playing Sabrina or My Fair Lady. I grew up fascinated by her femininity, beauty and wit.

You can also pick someone you admire from any area of life, like business, politics, fashion, sports, culture, art, spirituality and religion, someone from your country or from abroad, who is living today or lived in the past, no matter how far back.

Take a few minutes to write their names down.

Some of the people I work with take less than five minutes to think about who their five guests will be. Very few people, less than five in hundreds, couldn't complete the list and only found two-three names even with more than five minutes to think about it. Damian wrote their names down in less than a minute.

So, who are they? I asked.

This was Damian's list:

- American talk-show host Jimmy Fallon
- Ryan Seacrest
- Jack Killian – the night radio talk show host in Midnight Caller, the TV series
- Delilah, the American Radio host
- Jim Carrey

Now that you've written down the names of your five guests, I told him, *here's the next instruction:*

You will be discussing one topic, one theme with each of your five guests. Because you'll be spending together 365 dinners, you will have enough time with each of them to find out everything there is to know about that particular topic they each master. Please take a few minutes to decide what topic would you like to discuss with each of them? Think that each of the people or characters on your list knows something very well and they could share that with you or even teach it to you. What topic will you be discussing with each of them?

Outside my office window there was a Christmas tree, still full of two-month old decorations. Damian fixed his gaze on a Santa Clause that a neighborhood cat tried to decapitate just a few hours before, unsuccessfully, because I scared her off. After a couple of minutes, he wrote:

I'd like to ask Jimmy Fallon how he found the strength and determination to only focus on getting to be on SNL (Saturday Night Live) and live every day of his high school life with that purpose in mind.

Ryan Seacrest…how did he get his first internship at Atlanta Radio Station when he was in college and what were his most important lessons there?

Jack Killian ….I'd like to know the ins and outs of a midnight talk show where random people can share their life problems and where the host can create a safe and healing space.

Delilah…how to keep on reaching the listeners' hearts and how to make a music radio show always interesting

Jim Carrey…how to be funny and uplifting and always lift people up with a great sense of humor

He gave me the notebook and I mouthed the words as I read them back to him. I looked up and smiled.

I said: *You've now thought of the things you'll be discussing with each guest throughout the year. There's so much inspiration coming to you, and what inspiration does is awaken the spirit to have courage when leading the mind into action.*

Here's the next step of this introspective exercise:

Each of your guests brings you a gift on the very first evening, right when they meet you. After all, they are polite and well behaved. You decide what each of them will bring you, but there are some rules about that as well.

A guest can only give you something of what they have. For example, a spiritual person you admire would most likely be unable to give you a million dollars. However, the gift could be anything. It could be a physical trait, an emotional ability, any talent they have, an object they own, be it the manuscript of a book or their dog, even time with them is acceptable as a gift. Their hair color, their eyes, their strength. A participant once decided she would like pop singer Robbie Williams to give her 24 h together on one of his tours. Someone else wanted a special costume Elvis wore to a concert. I remember a client who wanted all the wine the Obama's received from other Heads of state.

So, Damian, I said, *take a few minutes and decide what is it that you'd like to receive from each of your guests. One gift from each of the five guests, so you will end up with five gifts.*

Here is my list of gifts, he said, reaching out his hand over the small coffee table sitting between us. I was so curious to see it, as I always am with the people I guide through this process. You see, the gifts people usually choose are healing; they have a compensatory effect in people's lives. They *make up* for what is missing.

Jimmy Fallon gives me his perseverance.

Ryan Seacrest gives me his knowhow about music and entertaining.

Jack Killian gives me his power to engage listeners and help them care about each other's challenges.

Delilah gives me her power to emotionally connect to the listeners.

Jim Carrey gives me his sense of humor.

How interesting one's path of affirmation is! For some, it comes with the high price of *fighting* for one's vocational path against the (well) wishes of his or her family. It is a high price to pay because it puts significant strain on one's closest relationships. A *good* person who loves their family feels conflicted between following the heart's calling and *disappointing* their parents or their mentor, or simply *becoming a burden.*

I didn't say any of these to Damian. His inner struggle was stirring his thoughts and emotions like a cocktail shaker, but I liked to observe that each time he put pen to paper, the words were almost calligraphic. Where there's clarity, there's order in thoughts and emotions.

• •

Ok, what a nice list of gifts, I said to him. *I know I told you in the beginning of this exercise that I was a good fairy. However, I am a capitalist fairy and, from the five gifts you received, I will take four and you can only keep one. Why don't you choose the one you want to keep and circle it?*

Immediately, he circled *Jimmy Fallon's perseverance.* He then circled it again, and underlined it.

Needless to say, the gift people choose to keep is the most important one to them at the moment. You see, doing anything in your imagination is *safe* and many coaching and personal development programs guide you through visualizations so that you start giving your dreams more clarity and your nervous system can begin **seeing** and **trusting** what kind of actions would be necessary for a "dream" to be brought forth into reality.

But micromanagement or focusing too much on each step can be discouraging for someone who is undergoing a big change. Most of the time, people need to gain more psychological power first, which we translate as courage. There is a wonderful Coach who created a method that truly helps boost courage, Burt Goldman. The Method is called Quantum Jumping. It is wonderfully laid down and it is both practical and spiritual, if I can say so. I do something similar with my clients when they go through several visualizations during the process of vocational discovery. The core concept of Quantum Jumping is that whatever you dream you could be, you already *are,* and all you must do is learn how to connect with that part of yourself *immediately and at any time you choose.*

So, according to Burt Goldman's method and wisdom, Damian already is a Radio host *somewhere.*

Let's move on, there's a little bit more to this exercise, I told him. Of course, it's very hard for me to stay neutral, not to be directive, especially when some people's gifts are so obvious and I wish they would simply be on their path, cut the drama in their life and move along with the work they were meant to do. But I contain myself. It was a skill I needed to learn, because no **one** being possesses the knowledge over another human being's path, except for that person. All I wish for is that my guidance brings clarity and order in their thoughts and emotions.

I didn't have to check my phone to see the time. I knew our session would be over in five minutes.

Damian, I said, if it were possible for you to switch lives with any one of the five people on your list, let's say that you could live their life for a whole year and fully experience being that person, who would you choose? Circle that name.

He circled *Ryan Seacrest* and when the pen stopped, the tip leaked some ink and the page wrinkled a little. He kept the pen down for a few seconds more, then, like knowing the writing was done for the day, he put the cap on and relaxed his entire body.

Great work, Damian, I told him. To finish the day, I am going to guide you through visualization. Have you done any of these before? He nodded his head *no*.

I will guide you through a visualization that will hopefully bring you closer to feeling how it is to be in Ryan Seacrest's shoes. I want you to take two deep breaths and relax. Close your eyes and keep your back straight. I am going to guide you to a state of deep relaxation. I will count from 1 to 10, and when I say 10, you will feel completely relaxed. **One**, *your scalp feels relaxed,* **two**, *your eyes and your eyelids relax;* **three**, *your jaw relaxes;* **four**, *your neck and shoulders feel relaxed;* **five**, *your arms feel soft and relaxed;* **six**, *your abdomen is relaxed;* **seven**, *your legs relax;* **eight**, *your feet are soft and relaxed;* **nine**, *your entire body is relaxed;* **ten**, *you are in a deep state of relaxation.*

Damian was fully relaxed; his right hand dropped the pen to the side, on the couch.

In your mind's eye, I want you to imagine you're sitting on a bench in a park. It is a warm morning and spring is just turning into summer. Suddenly, there's no more need for a sweater in the early hours of the day. It's quiet in the park and you can actually hear birds chirping. You feel so relaxed and their chirping almost turns into music. In front of you is an artesian well and the sound of the water is so refreshing. You're relaxed but not sleepy. You're just preparing to start your day of work. In your imagination, you suddenly look up and you see someone coming towards you. It's Ryan. You feel excited but you are centered as he comes near you and sits down next to you. That's it. Ryan is sitting right next to you. Take a good look at him. Don't worry, he won't feel uneasy. What is he wearing? Can you see the color of his eyes? Perhaps he has something to tell you. But he is not going to do it in words. Pay attention to his energy. Try to feel it. It's a warm, friendly energy. It's filled with wisdom from his life experiences, the many experiences he had as a Radio and TV host. Some were extraordinary and some were incredibly hard. He overcame many hardships. All that energy doesn't need words to be transmitted. All you have to do is be open to receive it. It's the purest form of wisdom. Take a few moments to just sit in the energy of his wisdom.

A couple of minutes of silence kept thoughts away from me as well. I continued speaking, slowly and softly.

Before he leaves, Ryan has something for you. It's a small object and he reaches out his right hand, opens your right palm and puts the object in, then closes it into a fist. You wait until he leaves and then you open out your palm. You are surprised by the gift and you are smiling. In your mind's eye, can you look at it? What is it that he gave you? Feel the object, look at it closely.

I could see a smile in the right corner of his mouth, his eyes still closed.

The visualization was over, I took him out of the relaxed mental state with the usual end words: When I count from 5 to 1, you start coming back and when I say one, you will open your eyes feeling refreshed.

Five, four, you are coming back, three, two, one. Open your eyes.

It was a trophy in the form of a golden microphone, what he gave me. It had "Radio DJ" inscribed.

Damian, what would you say is your main obstacle right now, preventing you to pursue a career as Radio DJ and host?

I don't have a clear financial path in front of me, he said. I don't have a life plan, a budget. I don't know what I would do if I wouldn't live with my parents anymore. How would I support myself? I want to register for a Broadcasting school, and there is none here, in our country. I dream of attending the Radio Connection broadcasting academy in New York City.

Would you be willing to look at the necessary steps you'd have to take to start on the path of professional broadcasting? Learn about possible scholarship programs, how to budget your expenses, search for part-time work opportunities while you study?

I definitely would, he said. I'd feel much better if I could go and speak with my parents after I have a clear plan that speaks their language, which is numbers.

Coaching is needed many times after a process of vocational discovery. Coaching is important because it helps you train your will and stay focused on your objective. In Damian's case, his dream became reality and he got a scholarship at a broadcasting school in America.

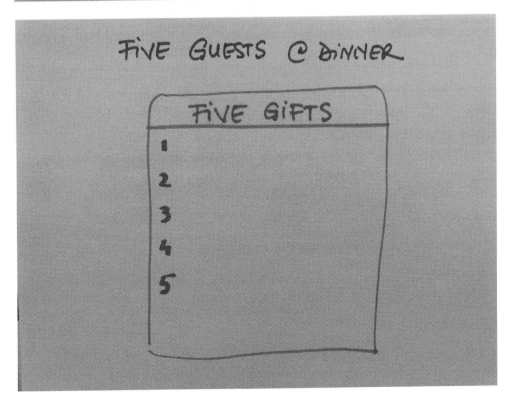

Chapter 3 – Mark and Understanding your Social Roles

Mark almost didn't come for his third session. I knew he was in therapy after his decision to get a divorce, and he was feeling overwhelmed by all the changes that had been unfolding during the past six months. But he was bravely navigating two big storms, or, better said, hurricanes: one in his personal life and one related to his work. They were both a long time coming, and this was the first thing he told me about himself when I met him:

I really don't like change.

Then, I got to know him better and by the second session, when he went through the *Five Guests at Dinner,* I was certain it's not change *per se* he disliked. He was just afraid *there was an end to love, when people left, and there was this void where everything became fragile and unpredictable.* He prolonged many situations in his life way past what was necessary or what could have been deemed a sacrifice, so that the moment of no return, the moment of *the end* wouldn't come.

He lived through such a moment at a very young age. His parents lived in Romania during the communist years. When he was seven, around the mid 1980s, his mother, a writer, *ran, deserted the country,* and fled to the United States via Paris, like so many Eastern European political dissidents. She couldn't take him or her husband with her and he, little Mark, didn't know. He just woke up one morning and she wasn't there anymore. He could tell something was wrong but his father and his grandparents kept on telling him not to say a word to his classmates or his teacher and that his mother and them would be reunited soon. How could a child live without knowing where his mother was? The night before she climbed next to him in bed and he could hear her sobbing and feel the warmth of her tears.

She didn't say anything to him, anything different, but that last night she didn't tell him a story, not even a short one. She was a successful writer now, living in New York City, on Roosevelt Island, with her German piano player husband and her daughter, his stepsister, a piano player herself. Mark began visiting his mother when he was 11, right after the Romanian Revolution of 1989 and the fall of a 45-year communist regime. He continued doing so every summer vacation until he turned eighteen and started college. When he was twelve, his father passed away from prostate cancer and his paternal grandparents, who had moved in with him and his father after his mother left, raised him from then on. His mother tried to *keep him* with her in NYC only once, when he was fourteen and he was getting ready to start high school. She had just re-married the German pianist and she was pregnant with a new baby. Every other week or so, she would be invited to an event in the City, to Boston or to Washington D.C. to read or to speak. She also taught Classical European Literature at a college in Brooklyn. The newspapers wrote about her and her talent. They congratulated her for having the courage to flee the country whose regime almost had her killed because of her opinionated poetry and short prose.

There were two writers on Mark's *Five Guests* list: Feodor Dostoevsky and Ernest Hemingway. The other three were some of the most renowned businessmen of today's contemporary world. *Two guests from his mother's world, and three from his, I thought.*

Mark had been a finance specialist and top investment advisor. People trusted him to always have their back, to take good care of their money, reputation and build them a sustainable and stable portfolio that would be crisis-proof. Yet he chose Hemingway as the one guest he would have wanted to trade lives with…almost the perfect opposite of the life he had been living. The changes, the uncertainty, the risks…Mark never took such risks in his life.

Yet these two changes in his recent middle aged life had been unfolding for some time, their slower pace making the shifting reality manageable to him, with help from his therapist. It was her that referred him to me. One of the things she told me when she briefed me was that one of Mark's beliefs was that *writers and artists in general tend to leave people and places. They get bored, need new experiences, can't be trusted.*

I'm glad you made it to this session, I said to him. I was surprised to see him wearing a T-shirt as he had always been wearing office attire before. He was tall and slim, and, just like in that Serbian childhood story, "The Emperor's Laughing Eye and Weeping Eye", his eyes were telling the same. His whole being was impressed with the energy of sadness, yet, somehow, I didn't feel it was something that needed to be fixed. That was how he was carrying himself; he had a calm and kind energy, dignified and a little sad.

Today's work will bring everything you've done so far into a new place, to connect the dots with what I call Your Social Roles, I said to him, once we exchanged a few pleasantries about our children and took a couple of sips from the Ethiopian specialty coffee I made before he arrived.

You know how we sometimes joke about some people having multiple personalities? Let me tell you that we all have, not multiple personalities, but multiple (and different) social roles. I want to make sure you understand this concept because it is crucial for all the discovery work you will be doing moving forward.

To clarify the concept of Social Roles, Mark, I will tell you a story. Here, I hesitated for a moment. When I tell this story to exemplify the concept of social roles, I use a man's story when I work with men, and a woman's when I work with women. This time, I let Irene's story introduce the concept to Mark.

Let's imagine a woman, we'll call here Irene. Irene is a 40-year-old bank manager. She has recently become a first time mother and her baby boy has just turned one. Let's say, for the sake of keeping our example in the realm of possibility, that Irene lives in a European country where she was able to have a paid maternity leave for a full year. She is now out of her maternity leave and has just started going back to work. I want us to imagine Irene's life for a moment.

It's 6:30 in the morning and Irene wakes up. Her husband is lying next to her in bed, still asleep, and she softly sneaks out of her bedroom. She enters the baby's room and her son is just waking up, reaching his arms out to her and babbling the sweetest baby sounds, and, of course, saying the sweetest word a woman can ever hear: **ma-ma***, said in a baby's voice. Irene picks the baby up and kisses him, talks to him softly and they cuddle for about twenty minutes. Irene has to go to work, so let's say that the nanny arrives in time for her to do her makeup and get dressed for work. Remember, she works in a bank and she puts on an elegant outfit. A year into maternity leave, Irene has gotten used to wearing casual outfits and almost no makeup. But, today, she takes about thirty minutes to get ready for her "bank manager" role. She leaves for work at 7:45 and gets there at 8:30 am. Her day looks like this going forward: she has a meeting with the senior employees of the bank. She is friendly but composed and she uses a more technical language, filled with financial terms; later in the day, she has a meeting with a potential client who would need wealth management services; she is professional, knowledgeable, and convincing. At lunch break, she goes out with two of her women colleagues that she has also developed a friendship with throughout the past years. While they walk, on the way to a salad bar, they laugh and talk. You can imagine, just by looking at them, that they don't discuss financial terms and work. Later, after work, Irene goes home and, because she has been very lucky, finds her* *husband making dinner (let's imagine her husband is a Chef) and the baby happily crawling and playing around them. She is grateful for her family, loving towards her husband and her baby.*

But, for several weeks now, something has been giving her insomnia. She finds it harder and harder to fall asleep. You see, Irene has recently come to see me because she wants to make an important decision. As the end of her maternity leave got closer, she realized she was feeling anxious about going back to work. She and her husband decided this was the only child they will have so the thought of spending as much time as possible with her baby boy kept her up at night. She began thinking of quitting her job and spending more time with her baby.

The reason she came to see me was that, after weeks of pondering about it, she decided that she will quit her job and will need advice as to an investment she could make. A friend of hers wanted to open a café while a former colleague had just opened up a Montessori daycare and needed investment. She saved up some money and was considering both options but wanted guidance in her decision-making process.

Here, in this story, we shed light on the concept of *Social Roles* and how they determine the decisions we make and the conflicts that often come up in our lives because our social roles can have conflicting goals at times. Remember, in the beginning of the story about Irene, I described her morning in a quite domestic way. We were able to see her in her role as **mother of a baby**, then as a **bank manager**, then a **friend**, and as a **wife**. In each of these roles Irene used different words, had a different mimic and gestures, and was even dressed differently. Of course she is ONE person; however, one person will act, look, talk and even think different thoughts depending on which role one is playing at the time.

Let's say you're in high school or college; you're in class and the professor is giving a lecture. Your *mind* is not there, not listening, because you're thinking of that soccer game you'll be playing after class with your friends. Physically, your body is in one place, but your mind in another. It's very hard to get things done when mind, body and emotions do not all align to support the activity of one role only.

So here's what I invite you to do.

Let's go back to the beginning of Irene's story. You remember I was telling you she came to me to decide whether she will put her savings into a café or a Montessori daycare after she quits her job. But my job with any person I guide through decision making is to help them understand WHICH role is most entitled to make the vocational decision.

You see, Irene has at least four major social roles she goes through every day of her life: **Irene the mother, Irene the Wife, Irene the Bank Manager, Irene the friend**.

Apparently, Irene wants to quit being a Bank Manager to spend more time being Irene the mother. But again, who should be entitled to terminate, modify or significantly change a certain important role we play in our own story? If I asked you, which Irene (which of her roles) is the one who came to me to ask guidance as to which business to invest in after quitting her job, what would you say? Take a moment to think about it.

As I progressed through Irene's story, I could see Mark being to fidget. The words change, quit job, baby, made him restless. I saw it and I kept going, taking the story to the pit stops where the fuel comes from the client's own realizations.

Irene the Mother, he said, in a dull voice. Irene the Mother wants to spend more time with her baby and decides to fire Irene the Bank Manager from Irene's life stage, at least for the foreseeable future, and make Irene the Mother the main character, with the most time on stage, he added, like he was looking forward to the end of this exercise.

And do you think that's fair, I asked? You could say that becoming a stay-at-home mom after two decades of working full-time may be the right choice for Irene. But accurately perceiving one's life at the moment of making important decisions means **defining** which role is entitled to make that decision. Which role of hers *should* make it? Let's look at it like this.

Let's compare the two roles from the perspective of **time and life energy** Irene has put into each.

Irene's Baby is one year old. So Irene's role as Mother is 1 year old too. For the last year, Irene has been living her new role as mother, with its emotions, thoughts, physical and hormonal changes. It has certainly put things in perspective for her, added depth to her life and a new meaning. But does that mean that Irene the Mother is entitled to end the career of Irene the Bank Manager to achieve her objective of spending more time with the baby?

Let's look at Irene the Bank Manager. She was, in fact, born twenty six years ago when Irene went to an economic high school. At the age of twenty two, Irene enrolled in a Master's program in Business Management and at thirty eight, right before getting pregnant, she was promoted Bank Manager. Irene the Finance Specialist, Irene the Vocational one, is twenty six years old.

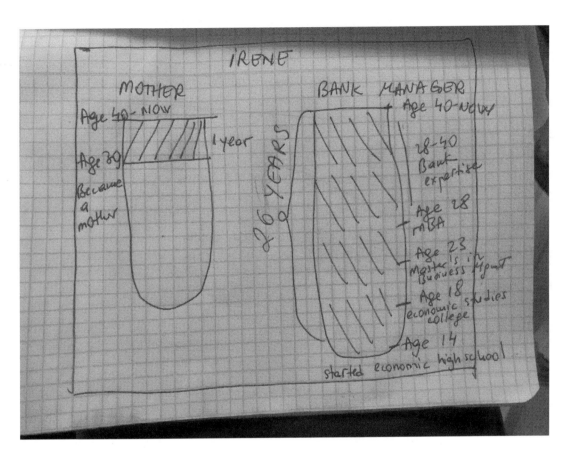

Shouldn't Irene the Bank Manager be the one deciding the future of Irene's career?

How can Irene know that six more months at home with her baby, full-time, won't make her intellectually restless, after a lifetime of mental stimulation? What if Irene the Mother and Irene the Bank manager would negotiate a temporary change in how much time each role occupies in Irene's life?

Instead of firing Irene the Bank manager for good, perhaps, with all her expertise, Irene can create a work schedule change for the next one-to-two years, until her baby goes to daycare. She could work a day or two from home, she could get Fridays off, she could renegotiate her pay for a more flexible schedule, or she could temporarily give up her managerial role and become a senior consultant to her organization. Multiple options are available the moment you understand that your vocational life is connected mainly to one of your roles but it affects all the others. Irene the mother, Irene the wife, Irene the daughter or the friend will not live, grow or fully support the objectives of Irene the finance specialist unless those don't come in direct conflict with **their** objectives. But all Irene's roles can benefit tremendously by her being vocationally fulfilled. You should remember that each role we have has its own objectives, its own agenda.

*Mark, we are here to discover which of your current roles is the main **seeker** when it comes to finding your vocation, assuming that what you told me when we first met is accurate, that being a finance specialist is not what you're meant to be doing with the rest of your professional life.*

So, for that purpose, I ask you to take a minute and write down at least four of your most important roles, the ones you play almost every day.

During our first session, he started writing in a Moleskine notebook with brown covers. His writing was very small, collected, as if he didn't want to waste the page. But he wrote the four roles extensively, both long and wide, until they filled a page:

- **Mark the dad**

- **Mark the husband**

- **Mark the financial consultant**

- **Mark the friend**

Obviously, Mark the son was not on his list, but I didn't say anything to him. In a way, it was logical for it to be elliptical, because the biggest roles are still the ones in which we put the most active time of our lives. We can assign emotional weight to a role and not give it active time during the day. For example, the role of the one who dreams of having another profession, the role of a lover who is not with his girlfriend, the role of a child living far from his parents and missing them. They become *daydreaming roles, parallel reality roles*.

Although the daydreaming role does not manifest itself in actions during the day, it comes and takes another role's time, occupying our thoughts while we are supposed to do something else. In this way, we can physically be in the role of a professional at work, but let our thoughts keep flying back to a part of ourselves that plays the guitar or runs an animal shelter. That's why it's so important to remind our roles, like a director, what scenario they have to play and at what moment in the play. Some call this controlling your thoughts and emotions well enough to have constancy of the right actions.

Conflicts between roles are always the cause of anxiety and sometimes even cause depression. Unfulfilled roles end up sucking out the joy from the other roles too. Most of the time we say that when the reality of a certain role and the expectations we have for it do not match, that is what causes depression. But I think that depression can occur when one of our important roles that wants its time on stage is permanently suppressed. That role also has its own needs and objectives. *And our vocational role is a main role, not a secondary role, Mark*. It is the role in which we spend most of our life energy on earth and in which we invest most of our internal and external resources, mental, physical and emotional, throughout our lives, ever since our teen years and long after our kids have grown up. This role does not exist just for us to provide financial stability to our other roles, such as that of parent, son, friend, and lover. **It is a leading role**. A psychological proof that this is true has been demonstrated through scientific studies on life expectancy and life quality of retired people. Suddenly ceasing to be a working person induces great psychological and physiological changes, for the worse.

I could hear Mark think of his mother by the sudden movements of his hands and the restless facial expressions. He blinked often, bit his lips, raised his eyebrows, played with the wedding ring on his finger. Maybe he was wondering which role of hers had left him at the age of seven. Which role did his mother try to save or which role did she prioritize when she fled the country? Maybe it was the writer/political dissident, the vocational role that was certainly the strongest role of his mother's life, that ran away from him and his father. Maybe *the mother* was never a main role to her.

There is no greater responsibility than that of a parent towards the stability of his children's lives, he told me in our first session, when he told me why it was only now, five years after deciding it was time to **make a career change,** that he begun, with cautious steps, disengaging from responsibilities in the world of finance.

His role as father prevented him, until now, from making any changes regarding the other important roles in his life, the role of husband and financier. Mark's relationship with his wife hadn't been working for many years. Now, both aspects of his life were undergoing big changes.

This happens to many people. To the majority, I would even say. There are few who discover and realize, early on, that when the professional role is vocational, when it is suitable for mind, soul and body, it becomes the source of power for all other roles, but also a standard of authenticity. I have yet to see a man who is not authentic in his profession, but he is so with his life partner and children.

When you are authentic in your profession, happy with whom you are and your gifts' expression in this world, you are generous, you are understanding, you are loving and you are kind. None of these are truly possible if your dislike your work. It is the same thing as disliking yourself.

I talk a lot in my sessions, and I know it comes from my vocation as teacher. I was born to speak, write, teach and give guidance or counsel. This is where the vocational spinning wheel stopped for me, my lucky 21.

Would you say Hemingway's path was vocational?

Of course, he said. *He didn't really care about anything else, he was a selfish asshole.*

But everyone on your list of Five Guests is truly vocational, Mark, dedicated to their work, breathing life through their work. Did you pick them because they were selfish?

No, I picked them because I admire them. I wish I had the luxury to be vocational.

Mark, can I ask you, if you were to look at which Mark, which of your roles, just said these words to me, whom would you say it was?

Hmmm, he said, biting his lower lip, *Mark the Father. Wait, no, it was Mark the frustrated Amateur writer. That's who.*

And how does Mark the frustrated Amateur Writer feel towards Mark the Father?

Like he should be more trusting, like he should give me a break to finally, finally, finally (he said the last **finally** in a higher pitched voice) *let me write!*

*Your mother gave herself permission to write…*I said, slowly. *Your mother is a wonderful writer, Mark.*

She is, he said, softly. *I keep this poem in my wallet,* he said. *I don't know when exactly she wrote it but it was published about two decades ago and she recited it at a literary circle when I was in NYC with her one summer.*

Would you read it to me?

Yes, he agreed.

Unconditional Love

The tall, slim, dark haired man

Made of gold rays and moon stone

Looked at me, slick and slender, but wild

Brimming with passion and holding it back until

Loving me became the explosion of everything that's right and wrong with him

It all collapsed onto the both of us like lava

Like an avalanche of words that were whispered, yelled, cried and shouted but never heard,

And his eyes, oh, his eyes

Finally agreed that

His reflection in my eyes is beautiful and needs no other background

Of color or sound.

He could watch it for hours on end

And there he could safely stay,

He need not be afraid anymore.

The Five people you put on your Dinner List, Mark, they are all vocational people, I said, about 10 seconds after he finished reading. I knew the poem by heart and I was a huge fan of Mark's mother. We never met but I had read many of her poems and short stories. Her love affair with the German painter and the life she had built in America after fleeing Romania were pretty well known in the intellectual circles, and not just in Eastern Europe. I never knew she had another child in her native country.

And you think vocational people should just leave their children or not give a damn about their family?

*No, I don't think that at all. But vocational people do prioritize that role and they do that throughout their adult life, in parallel with living out their other roles. When people go through the exercise of the Five Guests at Dinner, every single person on that list has prioritized, no, they **made** their vocational role their key role. That is why You and I know of them: politicians, actors, businessmen, sports people, and spiritual teachers. A vocation requires dedication, Mark. It consumes you; it is who you are at your deepest, most authentic level. It is the mechanism through which your gifts are best expressed and become useful in this world. But I don't believe your vocation should hurt your family either, because at the end of our lives, we hold on to the energy of what we loved the most: the people we loved the most and the work through which we loved and honored life.*

Then how do so many artists or businessmen or athletes do well with their work but are so bad at relationships, he asked. *Some were absent from their kids' lives, or cheated on the partners. But they are really good at what they do…*

This is not a question for one's vocational discovery process, Mark. That's more a question of personal values and virtues. We all make mistakes and, hopefully, we learn from them. We learn how precious it is to be appreciated and fulfilled in each of our roles. I want us to go full circle with the exercise of Social Roles so that we can move forward in our next session. I want you to discover one thing today.

Which one of your roles is searching for his vocation? Look at the list you made. Take a good look at it. Is there a "Missing" Mark? A role that is missing? The hidden diamond of this lesson is in connecting the *Five Guests at Dinner* with what you now know about your Social Roles.

The Guest you chose to spend a year as was Hemingway. Look at his name and ask yourself: out of your four roles, the ones you just wrote down, which one would best fit into his life?

None of them, he said.

That happens often when I guide people through this process. This is because there is at least one role missing from their list. It is a role they've probably given a lot of emotional weight to, but no active time on their Life stage.

It's Mark the Writer, obviously, he said. *But my question is, how? How do I make room for Mark the Writer in my life? I have so many responsibilities! You said it yourself in the Irene story: I already put over 20 years of my time and resources into Mark the Financial Specialist. Mark the Writer could never be Mark the Provider.*

Oh, I said, here's another important role in your life you should take a closer look at. It seems to me like Mark the Father, Mark the Financial Specialist and Mark the Provider are teaming up against Mark the Writer. But you did well, you have someone on Mark the Writer's Team, and you made it here.

*It's just that I don't want to overly romanticize being a writer. I want to write, I want to grow this part of myself but I don't know if it will ever be possible for me to **only write**, like my mother does.*

*What do you mean when you say **to only write?** Are you comparing the value of being a writer, spending one's life as a writer to having perhaps a more practical type of work? And do you know how your mother lives off of her writing?*

It's probably more complex than I think, he said.

A role you do not know is always more complex than you think. Can you at least think of all the things she does for her writing to be sustainable?

I know she writes for two magazines each month, social op-eds. And her books, her short stories, she must make money off of those. They received some international prizes, he said.

I sensed pride in his voice, and it was personal, a son's pride for his mother's success.

*She teaches college kids, I guess that's her main day-to-day job. And she goes to events, she gives speeches. She even did a few TED talks; I think one was in Toronto just a few months ago. And she's in her early 70s but is still working every day. I know for a fact that she writes **every single day**.*

I see, I said. It sounds to me like writing is very serious work for her. Can you imagine your mother being anything else but a writer, Mark?

Absolutely not, he said. *I think she was first a writer, and then she was my mother.*

What about you? Can you imagine Mark being something else other than a Financial Advisor?

Oh yes, I do that all the time. I imagine bits and pieces of that life all the time, every day.

But there's one thing you don't do every day, is it?

What, he asked, *but immediately knew the answer, so we both said it:*

Write.

The truth is that we leave behind a legacy. Almost each one of the people on my clients' lists, the people on your list, if you've made one already, they left a legacy that is connected to their vocation. At some point in their lives, each of these people gave their vocational role enough time and life energy to allow it to grow and serve other people around them.

And almost all the Five Guests at Dinner, on all the hundreds of lists made by people going through this method, practiced their vocation a long, long time. Of course, they were talented, you could say. They were lucky, they were successful. All these are true.

And again, the factor of life-long commitment to a vocation comes up. How could you be sure, once you discover that line of work that you feel inspires you and suits you, that you will be able to practice it for a long time?

In the next Chapter, and through Margaret's story, you will be introduced to the Vocational Triangle, a highly useful Clarification Tool and the crux of my vocational discovery method. It will help you create a personal framework that will allow you to check with full confidence if a profession could be your long-term vocation.

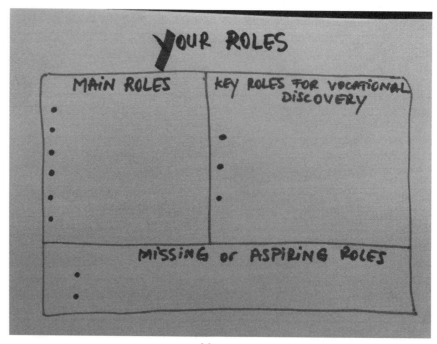

Chapter 4 – Margaret and the Vocational Triangle

Margaret wasn't meant to do one thing or to play one part for a long time. She was beautiful, lively and full of herself, carrying herself with the ease and unintentional arrogance of a sixteen year-old. A good friend who worked for the Mayor's Office received her resume one day as she applied for the position of Spokesperson for the Cultural Office. He never saw a resume like hers and thought I'd find it interesting. I did, and I got to meet her, too.

At thirty six, Margaret had been a fashion journalist, an actress, the creator of an independent theatre company that put on summer camps for high school kids and, most recently, an art therapist. But something had happened (yet again!) and she was now looking to work as a Spokesperson for a public institution. That would be such a big change in her life! What got my attention was the fact that she seemed to be fairly good, if not very good, at all the things she did, and she stayed with each career for at least three years since graduating college with a major in sociology.

It took a while to unravel this vocational mystery and I did, thanks to the Vocational Triangle. In fact, it was Margaret herself that did it, and her story helped me refine the tool even more.

Was Margaret a Renaissance woman, a polymath? Or was she still looking for her vocation? Why was she changing professions or were these even professions to begin with? Perhaps hers were a list of hobbies she took to an almost-professional level of practice.

I don't think there's hope for me, she said smiling ear-to-ear. I am the ever-teenager. I will never lose my curiosity and joy for life. I look around and I see my friends so blaze, so bored with their jobs, hating to go to work, doing it just because it's what society expects of them. I love what I do! And I believe a person can be very good at several things, not just one thing.

I agree, I said. Tell me more about yourself. I'm curious because obviously you've been blessed with a wealth of talents and abilities.

An only child, Margaret had been her parents' pride and joy since birth. Her mom was a day care teacher and her dad a deputy mayor in a small, provincial town. They had big hopes for her. Her story gave me hints that I immediately put together, showing me how each of my clients (or, in fact, any person) **frames** their relationship with work and the role work plays in their life since their teen years.

I've heard so many things about work: the classic *it's a means to an end, that it defines who you are, that it's honorable, that it's not what you do that matters, that you are not what you do, that it's what adults do to contribute to society, that it's a capitalist invention to keep us enslaved, that work has to be hard...*you have had your share of beliefs about work that you grew up with.

After weighing and analyzing my own beliefs about work, and observing how they affect the lives of other people, I drew this conclusion: our work *could* be the way we show up in the world. The way we show ourselves, our abilities, our dreams and our inner being externally. Our spouse, our children, know parts of us intimately. They would say **they know us well.** What about the rest of the world? Unless we're Barak or Michelle Obama, it is very unlikely that parts of our story, of our lives, would touch so many other people. So our work is an instrument through which we can show people outside our immediate family circle, what it is that **we are made of, what our emotional and mental gifts are.** There is no greater investment we can make but in ourselves – in the wellbeing and growth of our minds, emotional strength and resilience, and the health and wellbeing of our body. Because it is through these three tools (our mind, our body and our emotions) that we serve those around us.

Getting back to Margaret's story and the Tool I am about to present, well, it was during the session where I explained the Vocational Triangle to her that a realization about her multiple careers came to me. It wasn't that she was a Renaissance woman with many talents, all vocational. The truth was that Margaret hadn't really found her vocation yet. All the professions she had before met some of the conditions that define vocation, but not all.

She became enthusiastic when a new professional opportunity mirrored some of her key abilities and a new type of lifestyle she may have been attracted to for a while.

What the Vocational Triangle does for people who *could do several things well* is that it operates like a formula or like a recipe. It takes specific data that is characteristic to an individual and overlaps it on each of the three variables of the triangle. These three variables we are looking at in order to determine one's Vocational Framework are: Abilities, The Lifestyle that is Beneficial to You and the People Around you.

In short, you will know you have found the work that is vocational for you, the work that matches your abilities and meets your deepest needs, when you will not want to change it for a long, long time. It will fulfill both your mental and emotional needs to grow, not just one of them or mostly one of them. The formula I created says that V (for Vocation) is at the intersection of Your Abilities, your Beneficial Lifestyle and the Variable called People around you which has two categories of its own: People Like You and People you serve.

But there is a factor that applies to all the three variables, in fact it is a condition for the Triangle to create a vocational framework fit for you. I call this factor **the 70% rule, or the super-majority rule.**

As long as your choice of profession allows you to use and grow at least 70% of your key abilities on a daily basis, it matches your Beneficial Lifestyle at least to an estimated 70% of how you imagine it, and allows you to spend at least 70% of your work time around the People that are right for you, you will stay in that profession long-term. A lower percentage for any of the three variables becomes a predictive factor that can indicate and almost guarantee you will want to change jobs in the short-to-medium term horizon.

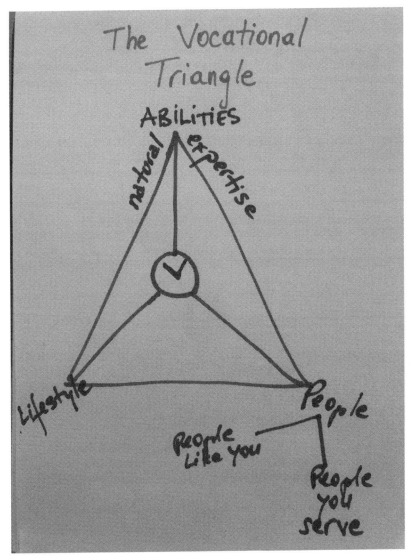

As I was explaining the Vocational Triangle to Margaret, it was her who said she'd like to test and see if any of the professions she had so far matched the 70% rule for all three variables.

It was the third time we were meeting and, so far, from her work through the other exercises, and especially working with her Social Roles, I remember she said this:

I don't like to be confined to just one thing. I am ten women in one; I can be a different character playing in a different movie or play every year. How else can life stay interesting?

When I work with someone, I don't try to convince them that the Vocational Path is the choice that offers one a more balanced life, or that it really is a life of greater or constant service to others.

You see, Margaret and many other people like her, believe that Life is a series of great and interesting experiences that we are supposed to gracefully and joyfully live through, as our existence on this planet is limited and passing.

One of my main beliefs, on which this discovery method is also based, is that Life was given to us so we can serve other people through our gifts. It is our duty to pay attention to those gifts, discover them, invest in them and grow them, and then offer them to the others.

But it was never my intention to prove Margaret's life vision wrong. She simply went along with the process and her "*a-ha moment*" came when she applied the Vocational Triangle formula onto the professions she held so far.

I was a model since my junior high school year. I loved fashion and I always dressed up. I still do, she said, smiling at me. I smiled back, having already complimented her on the wonderful black and white vintage Chanel jacket she was wearing that day, which she found for a bargain price in Paris.

I didn't really want to become a Sociologist, I really don't like charts and graphs and measuring people through numbers, but I really like to think and observe people's behavior. The modeling agency I had been working with since I was sixteen gave me a couple of modeling contracts in China. I was, at the time, thinking I could be an international model and go work with big designers in Milan or New York. One of my colleagues at the Agency, who was already twenty one, was a Sociology major and she told me it was pretty easygoing in terms of classes, it had an interesting curricula and the professors were nice. So that's how I got there, just to make sure I get a college degree, too. I loved the glam of modeling, the clothes, the jewelry, the make-up, the catwalk. College, for me, was really part-time. I had to find a job to sustain my expenses which had always been pretty high because I spent everything on nice clothes. I could really tell the difference between different designers, different styles, I could tell which spring collection a certain piece was from. The main problem with modeling was the environment, basically I didn't like being around those people. The designers I met were difficult people, very arrogant, and some made me feel like a mannequin that was only good for showing off their clothes. I didn't like most of my modeling peers either. They didn't have my intellectual preoccupations outside the modeling world. Other than clothes and make up, there was nothing I could talk to them about.

I was very lucky to make it to the NY Fashion Week one year, during the winter of my last year in college. I wasn't on the catwalk but I met an amazing fashion journalist who worked for the American magazine, Vanity Fair. I loved the magazine: it was witty, artsy and intellectual all in one! I realized that kind of world suited me more, and would still keep me around beautiful people and beautiful clothes, but I could also write and have smart conversations. After graduating from college, I got my first job as fashion journalist. It wasn't Vanity Fair but the experiences were interesting and I got to travel to Asia, Italy, France, several times during the four years I was employed.

In the end, I felt I had…consumed the experience. I didn't want to become Editor-in-Chief. I'm not drawn to managerial positions at all. I want to be as free as possible to express what I think and how I feel. But I could literally tell that **world** *was not where I wanted to live long-term either. Four years of it was enough.*

As she was talking, I was putting two and two together in my head. You see, Margaret was such a great example why the Vocational Triangle works so well. She was *somewhat* compatible with the Lifestyle of that profession, she brought some of her key abilities to it, and she partially liked the people she was working with. Like in an intimate relationship, we can be partially compatible, but after the *magic* of falling in love wears off, the excitement of the novelty of the relationship settles into a routine, *other factors* intervene to keep the relationship evolving instead of wearing down. And those factors are in fact mostly related to *social, cultural, spiritual* values and behaviors that manifest through actions and communication.

I was interested to learn what led her towards her next profession, *acting in movies*, which is one of the most vocational types of work. She only stayed in that *world* for three years and for such a brief career span in acting, she had enormous success: she starred in three national commercials and a short film which ended up getting an award at a prestigious international film festival. Margaret wasn't a professional actress, but she had the *personality* for it. Pretty, outgoing, outspoken, she loved being the center of attention. As Lady Luck would have it, one of her friends ran an advertising agency. The Agency was making a commercial for a coffee brand. It happened to be Margaret's favorite coffee and she was a coffee aficionada, she *knew* pretty much everything about coffee.

My friend just casted me in the coffee commercial and it turns out the client loved me. I ended up spending about a year in the advertising world and I shot two other commercials, one for a set of women's vitamins and one for a bank loan product for women entrepreneurs. I liked the fuss and the attention, even more than the catwalk. And then came the opportunity to star in the short film. The main character of the film was an Eastern European painter who sells his paintings, mostly nudes, to a famous but not as talented American painter who then sells them under his name and ends up making millions. I played the Eastern European painter's muse. I didn't have too many lines, but like the director said, the lines were in my eyes. I loved the role. I could have totally been a painter's muse.

It sounds to me like that could have been the beginning of a successful career in the film industry, I said.

It just has a lot of downtime between projects, and there's a lot of uncertainty about when you'd get another project, a new commercial, a new movie. I don't like not knowing when I get paid. Both the fashion industry and the film industry carry financial uncertainty and I just don't like that.

After the short film received that award, I waited for another project but it didn't arrive. The director said it could take a few more months until a new short film script raises enough money to start filming, but I wasn't a veteran of the film industry. In between films, actors do many other things, like shooting commercials, acting on stage, even doing corporate events on public speaking and creativity. I had some savings but the money ran out in about three months. I was getting close to my 30th birthday and I had always thought that by age thirty I would have made it big time. When I was twenty, I thought I was going to be an international model. Anyway, that's how I started my small business, running acting camps for high school kids. A friend was the director of a private high school and I did my first two-week summer acting camp with the kids from that high school. It was so much fun and it literally saved me, financially. The idea worked so well, and parents recommended the experience so I ended up doing these camps every school break for two years. But no other film opportunity came...

I discovered something else in exchange...how much I enjoyed working with teenagers. They are my favorite people! Somehow my next idea came naturally – I wanted to get some sort of certification so that I can expand the type of work I did with highschoolers outside the summer camps. I registered for this Art Therapy certification. It was a two-year program but I finished it and I kept on organizing all sorts of art workshops for high school students, all the way to a couple of months ago. All in all, I've been working with teenagers for five years now.

What a beautiful life, I said to myself. There are definitely people who will not hold on to any one profession for the entire time of their active adult life. These people are defined by curiosity; they oftentimes have a certain (and healthy) degree of narcissic personality and think highly of themselves. Explorers need to find new challenges and conquer new territories once in a while. Margaret was like that.

But I was puzzled by the desire of working for a Public Institution after her long streak of entrepreneurship. Beaurocracy and hierarchy were not something she had ever experienced.

Of course, I wondered why she wouldn't expand her business, hire a couple more people, serve more high schools, and create more acting workshops. Somehow, to me, this seemed the closest to a vocation, in her case.

It was during my sessions with her, that I stumbled, so to speak, over the concept we've all heard of in personal development, called *fear of success*. This is not necessarily related to discovering your vocation, but it is related to one's capacity to stay in his or her line of work long-enough to become an expert, to truly make a difference, to explore that area inside out, to master it, teach it and leave a mark on the field itself. Among vocational people, not everyone will become a master or a mentor. This *ability* of the mind, to stay in a place long-term is called *commitment*.

Margaret, and many people like her, was unable to *commit* to her work long-term. I looked into the psychology of *commitment* because *commitment* means two things:

1. Choosing one thing over another without changing your mind

2. Staying in a career or in a relationship long-term, without feeling unhappy or constraint to do it.

John Meyer and Natalie Allen developed the theory called *Three Component Model of Commitment* and published it in the 1991 "Human Resource Management Review." The model explains that *commitment to an organization is a psychological state*, and that it has three distinct components that affect how employees feel about the organization that they work for.

The three components are:

Affection for your job ("affective commitment").

Fear of loss ("continuance commitment").

Sense of obligation to stay ("normative commitment").

I believe the same three components are at play when there is long-term commitment in relationships, but that is another discovery process.

In Margaret's case, long-term commitment had not been achieved in any of her three professional activities. She was on the verge of closing her small business and trying on another hat, for which in reality there might have been less of a vocational compatibility than it was for running workshops and acting camps for teenagers.

One thing caught my attention, though, when Margaret told me she applied for the Spokesperson position with that public institution. *Spokesperson* is someone who takes the stage and speaks of issues in the name of an organization. Margaret had lost the *spotlight,* her place *on stage,* which she had, both on the catwalk and in film. The workshop business provided her financial stability yet deprived her from using what seemed to be her key natural ability: to shine on the stage, to act, to represent.

Her story showed me that even though we learn things that we use in our work (and we call these competencies), unless our workplace offers us the possibility to use our most important *natural abilities*, we will feel unfulfilled.

Margaret's *recipe* meant, in her case, that her long-term professional commitment would be possible in a place where she would be allowed to shine on some sort of stage in an area that was art or culture or education-related, but which also gave her financial stability.

And above all the other natural abilities that Margaret had, the one to shine in public was the most important one to her. She followed that feeling, that emotion, in everything she did.

When we look at the Vocational Triangle, one of the three most important reasons why most people leave their job and change their career is related to not being able to use their key abilities on a daily basis.

If you are able to use only about 40 to 50% of your Natural Abilities in your job on a daily basis, there is a high probability that you will keep on searching for a better suited type of work where you can use more of them.

How many people you know come alive during their week-end and vacations, and paint, do arts and crafts, hike, study nature, sing? People refer to this as practicing their hobbies, but the truth is that these so-called hobbies are natural abilities that most people find hard to incorporate in their work, most of all because they didn't choose it properly in the first place. They made the choice of job unaware of the long-term consequences of being unable to use the majority of your natural abilities at work.

Margaret didn't get the Spokesperson job, and I think it was to her advantage. One's vocational Recipe includes a variable I call People Like You. Had she been employed at the public institution, she would have soon experienced finding herself among very different people than she, and, sooner or later, it would have driven her to leave.

Could someone like Margaret ever stay in one place for more than three-four years? I believe, yes. When maturity sets in, the other two components of work commitment, **fear of loss and sense of obligation to stay,** weigh more and more. The sense of obligation to stay doesn't have to derive only from the responsibilities one has towards providing for their family members. Morally speaking, we have an obligation to the People we Serve to do our best to stay in our profession, better ourselves to serve them better.

Chapter 5 - Lea and Natural Abilities

Lea was a sweet sixteen-year-old who had been playing the piano since she was five. Her parents sent her to me because she was facing a big change and they wanted her to be *certain* that playing music as a profession was the life path of her choice, not theirs. Lea was admitted to the Mozarteum University in Salzburg and was just preparing to move there, together with her grandmother, as her parents had two younger children and would not be able to join her full-time in Austria. With her move, it became clear that she was embarking on a musician's life, with all its rigors, challenges and satisfactions.

It seemed that, in Lea's case, she had discovered her vocation early on. Her father played the piano and her mother loved to sing. Music brought their family together in a way that nothing else would; not sports, not traveling. Music was *running* through their veins but, still, there was no professional musician in their family. Lea would be the only one.

On a sunny day in early May, about four months before she was supposed to move to Austria, Lea sat in my office, pen and paper in hand. Her list of Five Guests was two piano players, two composers and the opera character, Turandot. She, herself, seemed to be musical, as if an electrical current of elegance, poise and power was constantly running through her slim and petite figure, harmonizing her posture and maintaining the symmetry of her smile, both on her lips and in her dark green eyes. She wore no jewelry other than small pearl studs.

Her long wavy hair was braided that day. On the other days we met, she was wearing it down, with curls flowing around her eerily. She was not like any of the other teenagers I ever met.

Lea, I said, as I looked intently at her pen and paper, *discovering all your natural abilities and determining which ones are your* **key natural abilities** *is essential to making sure you found your vocation. We all have a multitude of abilities. We're all good at something; in fact we are good at several things. But some Abilities we have are inborn, or natural. They don't come to us because we learned them in school. Today is the day I will guide you and you will write down all your natural abilities.*

You haven't been in Music School full-time until now. Going to Austria to study music will determine not only a big change in your short and medium term future, but most likely be the most important decision of your life.

I know it is the right decision, she said, *in a soft and calm voice.*

And I believe you, I said. *You already are a musician. But today you will expand the understanding of your natural abilities. With vocational people like you, I find that one or two of their natural abilities don't develop as much as they can because their work is so specific and fills up their life completely. They constantly use a certain set of abilities and competencies.*

Abilities are not limited to Talents, and Talents are not limited to Artistic Talents. Many times, people I work with tell me they have no talent at all, by which they mean they don't think they have any artistic talent. A natural ability is basically anything that you do **easily**. If I were to ask you what is it that you find easy to do without being stressed about if I asked you to do it for two hours a day, every day, what would that be?

For me, it would be reading biographies, writing poetry, short stories or motivational articles, riding my bike or walking through a park or around historical buildings, singing and of course, listening to people's stories. I could do each of these activities easily, naturally, every day, without being stressed. Some people could say one of their natural abilities is to cook or to craft jewelry.

In vocational discovery, your natural abilities go a longer way and have a deeper meaning than you think. For example, cooking and making jewelry, playing the piano and doing nail art or make up, all belong to a category I call **manual dexterity**. You like working with your hands. It is a hint your body and mind is giving you about including working with your hands in the profession you choose. A little thing like this, called manual dexterity, can be the reason why, after ten years of working as an accountant, and having a small jewelry business on the side, someone decides to quit the profession they have invested over a decade and a half in, if we add the years one spent studying.

I want you to take a few minutes and write down the list of every natural ability that comes to your mind.

A few minutes later, I took her notebook and read back to her:

- *To play the piano*
- *To compose my own music*
- *To make all types of braids for me and my sisters*
- *To read travel books*

- *To take photos of flowers, trees and birds*

- *To make people calm and help them find inner peace through music*

That's a wonderful list, Lea. And, like almost anything in life, whatever you think you know about yourself and the world can be expanded and transformed. In this process of understanding why a Vocation is right for you, your Natural Abilities are the most precious gifts you give others through your work.

Now, we're going to add another layer of understanding which ones of your natural abilities are the most important for you to express in the world often, on a daily basis.

For that, I'll talk a little bit about the **three vehicles of our being**. Without going too deep into philosophy or psychology, I'll tell you that **we experience the world through our body and our senses, our mind and our emotions**. Being a musician, you know that already.

When we go to work, when we (hopefully) practice our vocation, the work we do must be beneficial to our body, our mind and our emotions, too. This will reflect more in another concept, another variable of the Vocational Triangle, that you'll be working on later, called your Beneficial Lifestyle.

Our natural Abilities, too, are divided into three main types, each corresponding to our body, our mind or our emotions.

If you look at your list of Natural Abilities, and we take them one by one, we can place each of them in one out of three categories: an ability of the body, an ability of the mind, an emotional ability. One ability can belong to two or all three categories simultaneously.

I want you to run through the list and make a note of the category each ability **mainly** belongs to:

- *To play the piano – mind (mainly), body and emotions*

- *To compose my own music – mind and emotions*

- *To make all types of braids for me and my sisters – mind and body (hands)*

- *To read travel books(mind)*

- *To take photos of flowers, trees and birds (mind and emotions)*

- *To make people calm (emotions)*

She worked swiftly and immediately caught the distinctions.

Remember, I said, in the previous session, I made the point, using Irene the Bank managers' story, that you have to make sure the right social role makes the decisions related to your Vocation? In her case, Irene the Finance specialist was supposed to lead the decision-making process about any changes in her long-term career.

When it comes to understanding all your abilities, it is important to know that every single Role you have has certain abilities which can come in handy in your work. In fact, all your Roles collect data from their respective interactions and relationships and that data is super useful when you want to serve the people around you through work that comes from your mind and your heart, too.

So, I'm going to guide you in expanding your initial List of Natural Abilities yet again. When we went through the Social Roles exercise, I asked you to write down your social roles – at least four important ones. To remind you, yours were **Lea the piano player, Lea the daughter, Lea the sister, Lea the friend and Lea the high school student**. *I'm going to ask you to take a closer look at each of these Roles and see if that particular role has any other Natural Ability you can add to the List. When you write an ability down, make sure you make a note if it is an ability of your mind, emotions or body.*

Let's take Lea the Piano Player first to see if she has any additional Natural Abilities you could add to the list.

Lea smiled. She wanted to be **Lea the Piano player** more than anything else. It was the most developed part of her, overwhelmingly informing her decisions. But Lea was now about to leave her home, her family, her loving parents. The change would be big, and even if it was the right one for **Lea the musician**, **Lea the daughter** and **Lea the sister** may struggle when faced with a new reality that wouldn't allow those parts of her being to express their abilities in the environment they were used to. Our vocational life has to make room, and not just a little, for the other parts of ourselves to grow and express their abilities: our ability to unconditionally love our family or to receive their love, our ability to unwind and listen to our friends. There has to be space in our lives, in our lifestyle, to accommodate the needs and abilities of our other roles, even if our vocational role takes up most of our time.

Her expanded list of Natural Abilities looked like this:

- **Lea the Piano Player:**

- To be patient (ability of the mind)
- To never give up (ability of the mind)
- To be graceful in my music and posture (emotion and body)
- Perfect hearing (of the mind)
- Great manual dexterity (of the body)
- **Lea the Daughter:**
  - To be loving and sweet (emotional ability)
  - To be helpful and work in a team with my parents (ability of the mind)
- **Lea the Sister:**
  - To be playful and generous (emotional abilities)
  - To work in a team with my sisters (ability of the mind)
- **Lea the Friend:**
  - To be funny and interesting (abilities of the mind)
- **Lea the high school student:**
  - To manage well my learning time for school vs. my piano practice time (ability of the mind)
  - To manage the pressure of exams and structure my study time so I am never behind (ability of the mind)

INITIAL LIST:

- To play the piano – mind, body and emotions
- To compose my own music – mind and emotions
- To make all types of braids for me and my sisters – mind and body (hands)

- *To read travel books(mind)*
- *To take photos of flowers, trees and birds (mind and emotions)*
- *To make people calm (emotions)*

Why is it important to categorize our natural abilities like this and to expand them? In this case, it is clear that most of Lea's natural abilities belong to the mind and emotions. So she expresses them mostly through her mind and emotions. If I were to check her list again, I would say that her natural abilities are best expressed through her mind, when she rehearses, composes, organizes her time, reads and takes photos.

It's important to know this about yourself going into Music University, Lea, I said to her. *It shows you that your vocation, which takes up most of your day, should allow you to work with your mind most of the time. Your Emotional Abilities are many, and there must be enough space in your day at the Conservatory to allow you to express and grow them. Right now, the family space, the family structure, allows you to naturally do that every day. But your new life structure must take that into consideration. Your mind's abilities cannot end up taking up almost all the time in your day.*

When you choose your vocation, you must use at least 70% of your natural abilities at work, on a day to day basis. But that means that you have to incorporate your key mental, emotional and physical abilities in your work every day, day after day.

Can you make a **top five** list of the most important natural abilities that you *know* you want to have space in your day to day life to grow?

She circled these five Natural Abilities on her list:

From the Initial list:

- *To play the piano – mind, body and emotions*
- *To compose my own music – mind and emotions*

From the Expanded list:

- *Lea the Piano Player:*

- *To be graceful in my music and posture (emotion and body)*
- Lea the Daughter:
  - *To be loving and sweet (emotional ability)*
- Lea the Friend:
  - *To be funny and interesting (abilities of the mind)*

If we are guided properly, we can all determine which ones of our gifts are so important to us to keep on giving. If the lifestyle won't allow us to do that anymore on a daily basis, we will try to restore a more harmonious one. These are, let's say, the ingredients without which we just wouldn't be ourselves.

Before she left that day, we talked about the other kind of Abilities that complete the Abilities variable of the Vocational Triangle: the Expertise-type. These are the more technical or knowledge-related things you learned, like mastering a foreign language, using a certain computer program, or being very good at a certain sport. Most people get hired for their Expertise-type of abilities. What's interesting is that, when people leave organizations, it is never because they haven't been given the chance to use their expertise. It is because there's not enough room or need for their natural abilities, or the lifestyle doesn't suit them, or they don't like the people they work with. Candidate interviews should of course look at expertise, but retaining a person in an organization, long term, can happen only if there's space and opportunity for the three Variables of one's Vocational Triangle to grow to at least 70% and beyond.

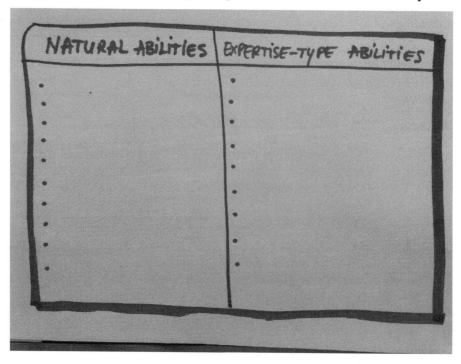

Chapter 6 – Sophie and Lifestyle

Sophie found this discovery session quite challenging. She had a lot of fun working with the other concepts, like Social Roles and Direct Utility and choosing the Five Guests at Dinner. But today she was challenging my view that the work you choose will ultimately dictate a large part of your adult lifestyle. Teenagers these days tend to believe that *work* is something you will *accommodate* in your life in such a way that your personal life, preferences, activities, won't be too impacted by the time demands of a job.

It's hard for most teenagers to even think that you could dedicate your life to a profession or to the service of others. The teen years are, naturally, the most individualistic ones, when young people begin to want things for themselves, to distance themselves from their family and integrate with a group of friends or experience the first romantic relationships. Separation from the *nest* is natural. The hardest time to tell your sixteen or seventeen-year-old that life must be lived in service of others through your gifts is right when they experience the opposite of that: that *life* is all about them. That experience is natural and necessary but this mindset has to be corrected, it has to be guided towards social utility. I believe it is the educators' role to do that.

I had to get this concept through to Sophie, though, because she was at an important crossroads. She was doing great in school. She had almost straight A's; she was great at math but also at humanities. She won several debate competitions so far. It had gotten into her head that she wanted to become an attorney. The first thing she told me in her first session was that she was going to be like Rachel in *Suits*.

One of the biggest problems with the college choices teenagers make is that they are completely unaware of the lifestyle a particular profession will come with. They have very general ideas about what a profession looks like, and that idea comes either from a movie or maybe from a family friend.

Imagine your teenager tells you she wants to be a successful lawyer and work in a big law firm, like Rachel in Suits. But she, in fact, is unwilling to put in the time to study and then work *over-over time* for the first probably decade after graduation.

This is where defining your Beneficial Lifestyle comes into play during the process of vocational discovery.

In the Vocational Triangle, your Beneficial Lifestyle is the second most important Variable. When work and personal objectives clash in a lifestyle you find too stressful to sustain, most often people end up changing their jobs, because of accumulated years of constantly falling short on time with their family and friends. The time you put into your work and the time for your family and friends must complement each other and replenish each other, not compete with each other. Most people I know (and probably most people you know) complain about not having enough time to relax with their family and friends or to pursue a hobby. And that is because they perceive their work not as their life's calling, but as a means to financially sustain their personal life.

Oftentimes, when they work hard at a job they dislike, people end up feeling resentful that family obligations keep them tied to that job. So, disliking your job can easily produce frustration and stress in your personal life, too. It is important to acknowledge that your choice of profession is never the fault or the responsibility of anyone else. It is in your power to do the work you love, and, in doing that, you will no longer count the minutes and hours you spend doing it, until the weekend comes, until vacation comes, until retirement comes.

In fact, your closest family members, especially your young children, can feel and see that you really dislike or that you really love your work. **Children are incredibly motivated by vocationally-driven parents.** In fact, it has been scientifically proven that parents are the greatest influencers of their children's career choice. There are so many papers and studies showing how this influence takes place, from the toddler years to teenage years.

Why is Lifestyle so important? I think we have to fully integrate the idea that work is an expression of whom we are and why we are here. Our work, like Kahlil Gibran said, is love made visible. We love the people around us through our work, so think about this: can we love the people around us if we dislike our work?

Lifestyle is the form, the framework for our life to unfold, to contain the expression of our work and the context of our most important relationships. Life is full of amazing experiences, yet our work and our closest relationships are the two *places where our most authentic expression can unfold.* We must create room for our work and our relationships to take precedence in terms of the time we give them, the attention and the connection that happen with being present both at work and at home.

Sophie was listening and I could see she was waiting for the practical part of the session to start. She was curious about her Ideal Lifestyle.

Sophie, I said, *in this session, you will be describing in detail what you think and feel your ideal Lifestyle should be. You're only seventeen, so I encourage you to imagine a day in your life five years from now, when you'll be twenty two, perhaps already a college grad. Some changes have taken place already, but let's imagine you don't yet know which college you'll go to.*

When you imagine your Ideal Lifestyle, let's only concentrate on its form. How does a day in your life look like at twenty two?

I will guide you through a short visualization to help you relax your mind. Let your imagination run free and, when you'll open your eyes, write down as many details as you can about the form of your ideal lifestyle.

It's a Monday morning, five years from today, I said, in a low voice. *And you love Mondays now; you don't dread waking up early anymore. Whatever your dilemma about your vocation was, it was resolved, and you chose the right path for you, the right college. You started on your vocational path. Your lifestyle allows you to naturally integrate your work and personal life and your days are filled with enthusiasm. You have a feeling of joy in the morning when you wake up and think about your studies and your work.*

What time do you wake up? Where are you? In an apartment, in the city? Perhaps further away from the city, in a suburb? Or in the countryside? Perhaps you're working remote and you're seeing the mountain green around you, or you're by the shore. Are you in your native country? Or abroad? Allow yourself to imagine the environment which surrounds you as you do this work that is vocational. Perhaps you work in a large institution like a hospital, the city hall, even a large political institution like the European Parliament or the United Nations. Let your imagination open new possibilities for you, be playful and trust that your intuition and your mind can work together.

What do you do after you wake up? When do you leave for work? How do you get there? By foot, by car, by bike or scooter? On the metro or the bus?

And when do you get there? What time? How does the place look like? Is it a modern office building? Is it perhaps an old historical villa? Imagine yourself entering the place where you do most of your work from. Is there any specific color your see? A painting on a wall? What is the painting of? Any particular fragrance you smell? Keep your eyes closed and allow your senses to give you information about a work life that uplifts you. What about the temperature? Is the air frisk, do you feel like going for a cup of coffee or tea? What do you hear as you enter the place you work? Is it the busy noise of several voices? Is it quiet? What about people's faces? Are there many people around you or just a few? Or is it just you in the beginning of your work day?

Imagine how the day progresses: are you meeting people? Are you on the phone or on your computer for a while? Are you perhaps not in an office, but moving across the city for meetings?

What are you wearing? In your mind's eye, imagine there's a mirror on the hallway of the place you work at. You take a look and you see your outfit. What do you see?

What time do you break for lunch? Do you take lunch at your desk or do you go out? What are you having for lunch? Using your imagination, think of what you'd like to have for lunch during this workday. It refreshes you and it is something you really enjoy.

What time do you finish work? What do you do after work? Where do you go? What activity or activities will add value to your day? Will you be meeting someone? What time will you be having dinner at?

Will dinner be at home or out? If it's at home, what will you enjoy more? To order or cook?

What about your personal life? Which parts of the day will you save to share precious time with your partner or friends?

Imagine, at the end of the day, being happy and proud of your work and of yourself. Imagine telling your partner or friends how much you enjoyed the day, the challenges of the day and the fulfillment you lived. There is no complaining, only gratitude.

What time will you go to bed? Is there a special bedtime routine that you have? Perhaps a meditation, perhaps a movie or a book. How will you end this day before going to sleep?

Slowly, come back, move your fingers, move your toes and open your eyes. Write down the day you imagined in as many details as possible.

I always read what my clients wrote in their notebooks back to them, in a loud enough voice so they can hear it. It becomes more real to them that way. It is also one of the key techniques in Transformative Mediation, which is a competency of mine, called Reflecting.

I wake up at 8 am and I am in the city. I'm in my native country and I live with my boyfriend in an apartment in a high-rise building. We have a small terrace and it's sunny and warm. We both have our coffee on the terrace. We study together and we leave the apartment at 9 am. I drive my car but we don't spend more than twenty five minutes in traffic. Before we get to classes I grab another coffee and we're in class until 2 pm, but then I go to my part-time internship in a big firm in the city where I work until 6 or 7 pm. It's very interesting, it's an international environment and I speak in English. The office is in a nice villa and I am surrounded by people from several countries. We talk about very interesting things, business, and politics. The office has a small garden and around 4 or 5 pm I finally have a little break to have a salad and absorb the sun for ten minutes. I leave at 7 pm and I meet my boyfriend at the gym where we work out until 8. Then we meet some friends at a terrace and around 10 pm we get home. I like reading before I get to sleep, or watch an interesting series on Netflix. We go to bed at midnight.

She seemed content with what I read back to her. Law school seemed like a good fit in this lifestyle that she described, although it was too idealistic for what the life of a recent law grad truly looks like right after graduating and joining a law firm as a trainee. But that is why I call this exercise the Ideal Lifestyle.

Once one writes it down, I guide them to expand it, to look at it from a different perspective, so that it becomes their Beneficial Lifestyle.

You are going to re-write your Lifestyle, I tell Sophie. *I know, you feel like you've done it already and it seems pretty motivational to you. Perhaps it is ideal or close to what you think is ideal. Remember, at this moment you are perhaps still unsure what is your vocation, which college to pick, what to do after high school.*

Your Life is not only a mechanism of accumulation, but rather it accumulates so that it becomes a mechanism of distribution of what can be given to others through you. I'm sure it's not the first time you hear that it is more important to give than to receive, but that is not the point here.

*When you re-write your Beneficial Lifestyle, you will not do it with **you** in mind as the main character living through your day, but thinking of your list of key natural abilities as the main characters. Do you remember which your top three Natural Abilities were?*

- *I am great at debate and getting people to see my side of things*
- *I am great at motivating others to be better or try harder*
- *I am very positive and joyful*

That's great! Those are extraordinary gifts that you must give to others through your work.

How must you live, how must your life unfold on a daily basis so that you can offer these specific gifts to people? We are going to do another guided visualization that will help you expand your Lifestyle so that it becomes a new possibility you can consider.

We will begin with an exercise I call the Treasure Chest, which is meant to help activate your intuition. I want you to keep your pen and paper close by, so you can write right after you come back from the visualization.

Close your eyes, again. Sit in a comfortable position, with your back straight and your feet touching the floor. Make sure your arms and legs aren't crossed. You need the body to fully relax in order for the mind to relax as well.

From this state, I want you to imagine you are in front of a mirror. You look at yourself and you see yourself dressed as you are now, in the present time. Right above your head there is a small ball of white light. It starts moving left and right above your head and you reach out your arm and you catch it in the palm of your right hand. It is soft and very bright. I want you to feel its qualities as you hold it. It is soft like marshmallow. And it is so bright but somehow you can look at it. The ball of white light is your intuition, guiding you to make the choices that create new possibilities in your life. It is finally able to answer the questions you wanted to ask so many times. But, this time, it will guide you to imagine your Lifestyle, the one that will allow you best serve the people you are meant to help in this lifetime, through your key abilities. Looking at the ball of white light in the palm of your hand, ask it this question: What lifestyle should I create so that I can help as many people as possible through my key natural abilities?

The ball of white soft light slowly and gently guides your hand to a treasure chest full of objects that you are just now seeing in your mind's eye. The ball of white light becomes one with the palm of your hand and it begins to touch some of the objects in the chest. There are hundreds and you can't see all of them very well with your physical eyes, but with the help of your hand and guided by its bright energy, you can feel the vibration of each object.

Some objects are shining more than others and you'd like to take them. What objects do you see? What got your attention? Keep those images, as brief or even as strange as they might appear, in your mind's eye. You will have to come back from this visualization but you are not coming back empty-handed. You are now holding, in the palm of your hand, three important objects for your life's work.

You will slowly begin to come back. Move your fingers and your toes, inhale and exhale deeply. Stretch your palms and your legs. I will count from 10 to 1 and when I say **one**, *you will feel fully awake and refreshed. 10, 9, 8, 7, 6, 5, you feel energized and refreshed, 4, 3, 2, 1. Open your eyes.*

As she came back from this visualization, Sophie looked at me as if she were a little surprised at what the intuitive mind can do. The intuitive mind takes over when we let our imagination run free.

Which three objects did you choose from the Chest?

Hmmm, I picked a book, a small book with gold covers, then a string of pearls and a small crystal ball, like the one you see in movies to foretell the future.

These are hints that will help you use both inspiration and the logical mind when you re-write your Beneficial Lifestyle, Sophie. You can actually do it a third time, in the next session, after you would have defined the last variable of the Vocational Triangle, the **People you Serve.**

But for now, I want you to think of how you can make sure that your Beneficial Lifestyle will allow you to constantly grow your three top natural abilities through your work. Before you write it down again, take a look at the three abilities and at the three objects you received in your visualization. Write them down side by side and see if doing this brings about any insight.

I am great at debate and getting people to see my side of things	A small book with gold covers
I am great at motivating others to be better or try harder	A string of pearls
I am very positive and joyful	A small crystal ball

She sat quietly for a couple of minutes and looked at her list. Then, she wrote.

It's about 9 am and I am wearing an elegant dress and a string of pearls. I am hurrying that morning because I am running a debate competition at my college, with first year students from other cities and abroad coming in for one of the final rounds. I am one of the seniors who organized the competition. This year the competition is about Girls and Women's rights and I have collected the speeches and published them in a booklet that will be sent over to a couple of Committees in the European Parliament, as inspiration for legislative change. After the competition is over and because I am in my senior year, I'm already working part time in an international organization. The purpose of the organization is to help empower women and girls to achieve their potential and we work with international organizations like the United Nations and UNICEF. At work, I am part of a team that helps young girls in poor countries find vocational work that can get them out of poverty and early marriage.

By the time I finished reading back to her what she wrote, I had teary eyes. **That** is the power of listening to your intuition. That is how much it can elevate your awareness about your purpose and your life, even at seventeen.

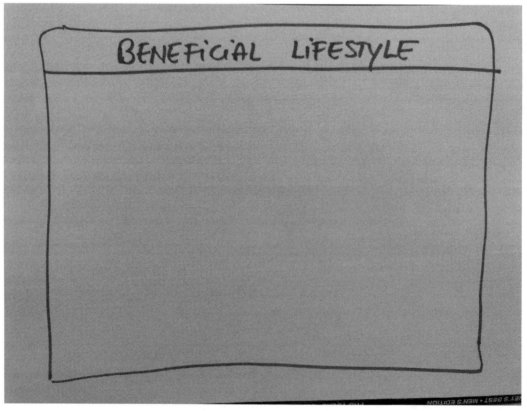

TREASURE CHEST

CHOSEN SYMBOLS / OBJECTS

-
-
-

You can also add your personal interpretation about what you think the symbols mean.

Chapter 7 – Dan and People Like Me

I never met a more entrepreneurial man than Dan. He unwillingly came to see me, because his business partner and he were getting ready to launch an online business that would eventually change their lives. He was a brilliant businessman, yet, other than his business partner and his wife, he was unable to sustain a long-term relationship with anyone. As their business began thriving, they had to hire close to fifty people. His business partner found that people management was entirely his job, and wanted to help Dan grow this aspect of his life. Dan created and ran various small businesses ever since he turned eighteen. He was now thirty five and this specific business was in fact very vocational and, unlike the others he ran so far, it was very people-centric. It also had a social mission, one that became more and more appreciated in the international business communities in Central Europe. It was an online part-time work platform that would bring experienced financial and tax specialists together and match them with international clients that needed the expertise of senior professionals while keeping costs lower than they would have been if the projects were given to international consulting firms.

Mostly women consultants would join this part-time work platform once they had become mothers and didn't want to work such long hours. Dan's business partner was a senior finance specialist, now retired, while Dan himself was an accountant by profession but his passion had been to build various online platforms for various products and services through the years.

Unlike before, Dan was all of a sudden to run a team of fifty employees, and the team was growing. He needed to travel to find the right people to join the platform. He needed to convince clients that the platform was a part of the future of work, where women-consultants with senior expertise would be able to truly balance their work and personal life. Dan claimed that he was an introvert and was happy left alone at his keyboard. In very rare cases, people really **stumble** across their vocation. He was so passionate talking about all the aspects of this new business, its social mission, how great the people on the platform were, but he was inflexible when it came to his role in the company. He would prefer *keeping* away from the *business of people* and just relate to *the online platform.*

So when he came to see me, this tall, blue-eyed man with a constant smile on his face, the first thing he told me was that *he is not looking for his vocation, because he knows exactly what it is, and he didn't want to change what he was doing.*

In fact, he told me right up front that he hated *babysitting* employees who needed pep talks and motivational trainings and *communication*.

It came as no surprise to me that one of his Five Guests at dinner was a Zen Monk. It was also clear that if Lady Luck gave Dan such an incredible idea which became successful way above what he could have ever imagined, it did so in order for him to grow his natural abilities to the next level. He was so adamant about limiting his in-person interactions with employees and clients, that I simply needed to check why he was holding this part of himself back.

Dan, I said to him, the third variable of the Vocational Triangle is People. You already know that, to me, it is the heart of the vocational discovery process. If I were talking to a future college student or someone who has just started working but wasn't sure which way to go, I would have told him that this is the most important variable. But to you, this "heart" part doesn't seem to carry the weight I'm used to giving it. Each of the three variables is giving you important hints about your long-term commitment to a vocation. Your Abilities are the gifts you offer through your work.

In your case, I know that both you and your business partner agree that the business you started a year ago needs a very different level of commitment than any of the previous ones had.

Yes, Dan said, *his main worry is that I will get bored with this business, too, and I'll want to sell it and start something new. In all honesty, he knows me for more than a decade, and, during that time, I started four online businesses, and I've sold all of them for profit. This, here, is different. My partner sees that we could take it to a big level, sell franchises after a while, but we have to grow this team, and this* **People** *factor gives me anxiety. I don't want to have to talk to many people or manage many people every day. I want to do my work from a beach in Greece, in front of my laptop, and spend the evenings with my wife. But he says this time it can't be like that.*

Dan, I really understand how dealing with many people every day may seem stressful to you. And I also understand that what you and your partner have created has a great impact not just in the lives of a certain category of people, women-consultants, but it really redefines work-life balance for women who are very senior in their profession. Somehow, this mission came through to the two of you.

Perhaps if you immerse yourself in this session and allow me to guide you, a different perspective could open up. As I told you when we discussed the Vocational Framework, the People Variable has two important categories we are going to look at: I call the first one, **People like me**, *and the second one,* **People I serve**.

You are going to define and describe each category in detail and I will guide you through it. Why is this so important? Because we have this saying: "people leave people, not organizations". And there are reasons why people quit their jobs even if they can use most of their abilities and even if the job provides a beneficial lifestyle. And that reason has to do with People, especially people who manage their work. You are in this position today.

Let's look at the first category - People like me. These are the people you work with, your colleagues, your peers. And in your case, their number increased 1000% in the last few months.

All of my own life experience and testimonies from the people I work with in counseling, points to the fact that we are happier among people like us.

Then, I would be happy sharing an office with someone who wants to spend his day quietly, just like me, Dan said.

If we are the odd one among others who are mostly alike, we won't be staying there too long. That goes for families, too, I added. *The odd one, the different one, the rebel one, will leave the nest as soon as possible.*

But that is happening at one level of awareness about one's vocation. There comes a time when vocation becomes intertwined with mission, and that mission may be bigger than your personal boundaries can contain. That usually means that you have to do your best to expand those boundaries and join forces with other people who share that mission.

But let's get back to the "people around you" as you are now expanding your boundaries about how people can become a part of your mission. Imagine you're a painter who graduated art school but got a job at a furniture showroom where he works with the décor, picks out fabric colors. At work, no one else does this kind of job. There are sales people, carpenters, unskilled laborers who move the furniture around, accountants, and some other staff. But he is the only painter, the only artist. How common is it for artists to get regular jobs after all, many times listening to all the noise around them saying that artists are always struggling with money?

It is likely that, in this example, the painter will feel the odd one out. He will blame his job for keeping him away from his art and will ultimately blame himself for working just for money. The job will tire him and he will not grow as a painter either. But if he wants to keep this job for longer, until perhaps he can open his own art gallery, he must integrate with his colleagues and he must immerse into the universe of furniture.

It is true that a more suitable job for the painter would be in an art gallery, in a museum, somewhere closer to the key elements of his natural abilities. But what if this particular person finds himself at the intersection of two fields: one is painting and the other one is furniture? What if the person is entrepreneurial and learns the management skills necessary to, in time, open his own art gallery or art shop that would include unique pieces of furniture? Mustn't he, then, familiarize himself with people from the world of furniture, of art, but also of business?

It's much easier to stay in a profession long-term if you put your abilities to work in a place where they represent the core work. Let's say you are an accountant in a theatre. You are surrounded by actors and directors and scriptwriters and stage managers and costume designers who probably dread talking to you. There would be a higher degree of direct utility for your work and you would receive better pay for it if you worked in a financial institution or consulting firm where you serve the client directly and the client buys financial services.

In the theatre, the final client is the audience, which is directly served by the actors and directors and scriptwriters, so you have a much lower degree of direct utility there. Sometimes, perhaps, you wish you'd have been an actor, too. But that may not be your soul calling you to be an actor, as much as your soul telling you to find your tribe.

Dan smirked. *What if I am not really meant to have a tribe? Perhaps my tribe is made of two other people. One, I work with, and one, I live with. I don't know too many other people who are like me.*

*Perhaps, Dan, you have taken on this challenge because in your case, the **People like me** category overlaps, in fact, with the other category, the one I call **People I serve**. Didn't you say that you and your partner created this platform because you wanted women consultants who have a lot of experience in their profession, to lower their time engagement at work and be able to still work with clients, remotely, while having a fulfilled personal life? How did you even come across this mission?*

*This, right here, is, to me, the most motivational aspect of the Vocational Triangle. The People you Serve are basically a mirror of yourself. The People you serve are a huge part of vocation; they represent the **why** in your mission to serve.*

Well, he said, *my wife and my partner's wife actually inspired us. Both our wives are consultants and they had been working day in and day out for at least the past decade. We basically only had time to ourselves on the weekends. My partner's wife gave birth to their son, three years ago, and she didn't want to go back working for the consulting firm where she held a senior position, because there would be no time for her role as mother, really. People in consulting know what I mean. She and my wife are very good friends and they began brainstorming for some sort of solution for consultants of their level of expertise to work more like independent specialists once they became mothers, so that they can continue to enjoy their work and spend time with their children. It's our wives that we wanted to serve, and our own families, first of all.*

That's very inspiring, Dan. Have you hired all the new employees in your company yet?

Not yet, we still have about half left to hire, about twenty five people. And I have to attend all the interviews with the short-listed candidates.

Well, have you thought about hiring those who most match your own vision as well as the company's mission?

You'll be spending a lot of time with these people, your colleagues, and your peers. Otherwise the company won't grow. For every person who works with me to discover their vocation or take on the challenge of a long-term commitment to certain work, which is what you are doing now, it is so important to figure out what qualities people at work ought to have in order for you to enjoy your work day instead of dreading it.

I want to help you become more comfortable with your new crowd, your People Like you. You have the opportunity to select them to your liking. Why don't you close your eyes and we'll do this visualization in a state of relaxation. Please sit in a comfortable position, with your back straight.

Take a couple of deep breaths. I want you to imagine that you are at your office and you're happy to be there. It is a sunny spring day and there's a spring in your step as well. As you begin your day, your colleagues join you. In your mind's eye, I want you to look around as if you were seeing these people who share this important time in their life, too, with you. Together, you serve other people in such a meaningful way!

As you look around to see your colleagues, how many people are there? Two? Five? Ten? More than ten?

You look at them and suddenly, there's a wand in your hand. I have just given you a magical wand. With it, you are able to transform your colleagues in the exact way you'd like them to be. You are allowed to make them a lot like you. You begin to use the wand and create the best colleagues you could ever have. One key reason you enjoy being at work is that you get to share that work and have your abilities seen and appreciated by your colleagues, too.

Please start imagining, how are they? Are they young, and if yes, of what age? In their 20s, in their 30s?

Are they all of your nationality or perhaps they are of different nationalities? Are they mostly men or mostly women? How are they dressed? Casually? In a more elegant fashion?

They are around you at your place of work but it's lunch break and you all talk about something else than your work. It's a relaxed atmosphere and you enjoy listening to them and participating in the conversation. These people also share some of your own interests. What are they talking about?

Are they sporty people? Do they love to bike? What kind of food do you enjoy having when you lunch together? What kind of music do they listen to? Or perhaps they love arts and culture, architecture and history. You share lots of things with them. They are not your close friends although some of them could be. But you spend so much time together with them that being likeminded and having a common vision will most definitely help you on your own vocational path.

Lastly, why are they there? What drives them in this work? What do they care about?

As Dan came out of this visualization, I asked him to write down what he imagined his ideal colleagues would look like. He wrote:

If they are like me, they will care about spending as little time possible doing bureaucratic, administrative things. They would love to use automated processes, AI, every possible tool to be more effective. They will be youthful and modern in the way they see society. They will care about work-life balance. They will have an inner drive to escape the corporate world and the 9-to-5 mindset. They won't spend more than five hours max in the office. If they do, they don't work effectively. The team has to be international and young, but not super young because you begin to understand commitment only when you have responsibilities. So, I want to hire people who have a family, they have a spouse or even small kids. They also must be passionate about the future of work. They must have a sociological mind, to be able to carry on a conversation that rises above the daily routine and goes deeper into how society will evolve when it comes to work. They must love to travel and also be experienced already in growing online platforms into communities. I want them to be mostly self-sufficient and not need someone to babysit them and tell them what to do each day.

Deep down, Dan was not a total introvert. His vision of life which he shared with his wife and business partner, led him to create this platform, and as he described the People he would like to work with, he, in fact, described his own values as well as his needs. When your vocation becomes a mission that surpasses your own life and benefit, nothing will carry it further faster than the power of many other people who share the same mission and thus, the same values. Values manifest as behaviors, in every person, which is why, if you know your values and can put them on paper, you will attract people who share them.

Chapter 8 – George and People you Serve

George was eighteen and had just started his last year of high school. He was a tall and slender boy with a pleasant disposition. He was very knowledgeable and seemed to possess a gift for storytelling. Each of his discovery sessions were filled with jokes. His mother was a brain surgeon and his father was a banker. His well-to-do family could have sent him anywhere to study once he decided which career he wanted to embrace. Yet he wanted to build and spend his future in Romania, his native country, where his parents worked, too.

In our initial session, I wanted to assess how strong his parents' influence was in relation to his choice of vocation. It was very strong, because he shared an incredible bond of love with his parents, but also admired them to no end. His mother encouraged him to go into banking because she didn't want him to live with the hectic schedule she had been living with all her life. His father encouraged him to follow in his mother's footsteps. Both his parents were vocational people and George grew up with the understanding of how it feels to be happy with who you are and with your work.

He was much more inclined to becoming a doctor and his natural abilities matched this particular vocation more than banking did. But there are doctors and doctors. There are so many specializations and the life of a pediatrician doesn't resemble in the least the life of a heart surgeon. George kept on talking about experiencing being a war zone doctor for a couple of years. I hadn't even heard the concept before, so we dug deeper to see why he was drawn to this. He was talking of specializing in reconstructive surgery and there was passion in his voice that was not coming from being persuaded. His intuition was giving him hints about his path.

But whose parents would want their child to work in war zones? So, here he was.

We've arrived to the heart of your vocational discovery process, George, I said to him. The People you Serve.

It was our second to last meeting and he had done very well through all the previous discovery work.

Today you will connect to the people you are meant to serve through your work, by using your intuition. I will guide you through another visualization to make sure you are in a relaxed state of mind and that your thoughts can make room for your heart to connect to its calling.

Not everyone is equally motivated to serve other people directly, to work with people every day. You are thinking of working with people who find themselves in a poor physical state, which is undoubtedly accompanied by poor emotional and mental states, too.

People's inclination to working in fields where they deal with people every day, as opposed to working in careers oriented towards non-persons, seems to be mostly related to the parenting style of their parents.

American psychologist Anne Roe, author of the Psychology of Occupations, discovered that children who experienced parenting styles she describes as "loving acceptance," "overprotection", or an "over demanding" style would be orientated towards careers with persons, such as jobs dealing with service, culture, or entertainment. On the other hand, children exposed to parenting styles of "casual acceptance," "neglect," and "emotional rejection" would be oriented towards careers with nonpersons, such as scientific and mechanical interests. However, about ten years after writing this, Roe abandoned most of her hypotheses, in 1964, suggesting that children pursued careers based on parental attachment. She then stated that children with secure attachments most often pursue person-oriented occupations, while those with insecure attachments do not want the person-to-person interaction too much.

But discovering your vocation is not just a thing of the mind, like I was saying in the beginning of our sessions. It is a little discouraging to believe that outside our parents' influence, there is little freedom of choice and little power to create our own future when it comes to our work.

George, I hope that, especially through today's session, you allow yourself to make this new choice, with as little attachments to the past and to your parents' preferences as possible. That does not mean you disassociate from everything you learned from your parents or from admiring their career choices. But do you remember, when you were younger, and at times expressing an admiring thought about a firefighter, a writer, an ice cream maker, a princess, you had your mom or dad minimize that admiration? By doing that, they also stopped an intuition which guided you towards the abilities expressed in that profession. Perhaps when you told your dad, at age 8, that you want to be a firefighter, he said, not meaning any harm: "well, son, they sure have a hard life. Better a doctor like your mother." Parents influence your career choice the most.

But if you're here now, it is because there is still some confusion about a few aspects of the work you are about to embark on. To clarify those aspects, understanding which kinds of people you are drawn to serve day after day, is key.

In this exercise about the People you serve, you must first give up the need to repay your parents' efforts to raise you by choosing a line of work they would approve of. You are here with a unique set of abilities and the power to create your life and your work. Do you know how many people become therapists, psychologists, doctors, lawyers, to save one of their parents or both? I am speaking metaphorically, in an emotional way. Or to continue their parents' legacy.

These sound emotional and I was there myself, making several decisions in my young adult life in reaction to what my father wanted or didn't want or to what he dreamt of.

But, unfortunately, most of the time, it turns out that creating our life to save our parents or our spouse, is a pit stop but not our final stop.

Vocational people are mostly oriented to serving key needs. They do so from a sense of contribution to other people's lives

There is a natural sequence of things when we serve people around us. We have to determine which one of their needs would we like to help them meet? If you look at Maslow's pyramid, what kind of service would you like to offer? Would you like to help people with their Basic needs, their psychological needs or with their self-fulfillment needs?

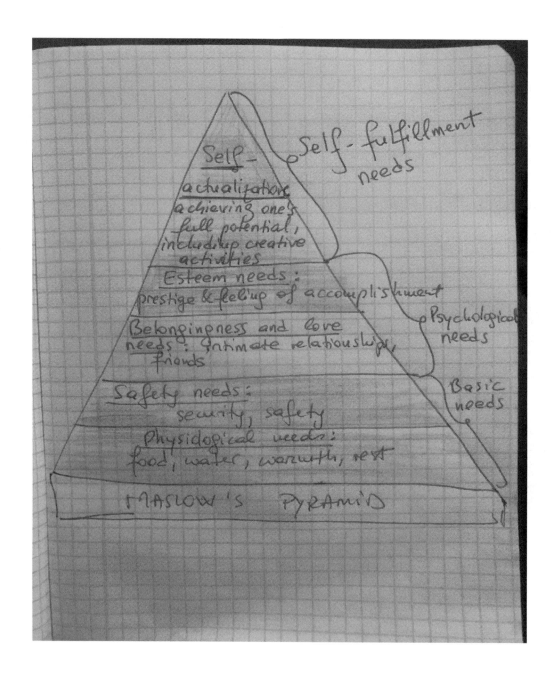

Lawyers and doctors, for example, help people mostly with their basic needs but they also must know how to contain their clients' and patients' psychological needs. Coaches, therapists, educators, help people with their psychological needs mainly. People who serve others with their self-fulfillment needs can be authors of inspiring books or programs, speakers, spiritual teachers, preachers. The higher the level of service on this pyramid, the more inclusive it can be of people from all walks of life.

George, I will guide you through a visualization that will hopefully bring you closer to the people you are meant to serve. When I close my eyes and I imagine a room full of people I serve through my work, I see teenagers and young mothers filling up that room. There is something you may call purpose connecting me to them specifically.

I want you to take two deep breaths and relax. Close your eyes and sit in a comfortable position. I am going to guide you to a state of deep relaxation. I will count from 1 to 10, and when I say 10, you will feel completely relaxed. I finished counting but I could see his body relaxed right after I said 5.

In your mind's eye, I want you to imagine you're sitting on a bench in a park. It is a warm morning of spring just turning in summer and, suddenly, there's no more need for a sweater in the early hours of the day. It's quiet in the park and you can actually hear birds chirping. You feel so relaxed and their chirping almost turns into music. In front of you there is an artesian well and the sound of the water is so refreshing. You're relaxed but not sleepy. You're just preparing to start your day of work. In your imagination, you suddenly look up and you see someone coming towards you. As they approach you, you realize it is someone you helped through your work, just recently. They come to thank you again. You invite them to take a seat next to you on the bench. Take a good look at them! Is this person a man or a woman? Are they young or more senior? Don't be surprised if instead of seeing a person sitting next to you, you may see animals, birds, tress, nature. Beings of all kinds need our abilities to serve. As you look at them, you are going to connect to your heart. Take a look at the person's heart center, in the middle of their chest. It is beaming in a bright light pink color. The color represents the gratitude they feel towards you. The people you serve are the biggest receivers of your gifts. This bright light pink color becomes a ball of pink light and it detaches from the body of the person sitting next to you. It comes right next to you and asks you to receive this energy of gratitude. You do so and you can see your own heart beaming with bright light pink energy as it opens to receive this gift of gratitude.

You are so motivated to continue serving the person in front of you! You feel energized and ready to start a new work day. Before you stand up to leave the park and say good bye to the person you met, they look in your eyes and verbally thank you for the work you do for them. Suddenly, more people show up around you. They, too, are people you serve through your work.

Although they are many, you can distinguish their faces, their features. What do you see? Take a good look around and connect with the people you give your abilities to. These are your biggest gifts and they are the receivers of these gifts.

Before you leave, you tell them that you will honor them by continuing to grow on your vocational path.

You will now begin to come back. Move your fingers and your toes, inhale and exhale deeply. I will count from 10 to 1 and when I say one, you will feel fully awake and refreshed. 10, 9, 8, 7, 6, 5, you feel energized and refreshed, 4, 3, 2, 1. Open your eyes.

Right away, I want you to take your pen and describe, in as many details as you can, all the insightful information you received about the people you serve. The information we receive through our intuition, when our mind in relaxed, may have come as sounds, colors, very short images, even words. Write down everything you remember.

He wrote: *I see older children, teenagers, like me, who haven't had my luck to live in a free and stable country, they haven't had my luck to go to great schools and choose their career. They are caught in the middle of political and economic conflict and they live in war zones or refugee camps. I see this boy; he is the age I am now. He speaks a little English. His clothes are torn and very dirty, his right cheek has been badly scarred and he is almost disfigured. He had dreams, although his immediate need is to flee from that area. I help fix his scar and I encourage him to keep following his dreams of fighting for his country's freedom. Teenagers like him are constantly saved and they are able to leave the conflict zone. Some go to America, some come to Europe. I can't be a bystander to the destruction of young people's lives. I am also involved with the United Nations and I contribute to educating future doctors on the importance of saving young people from conflict zones and help re-establish their dignity and ability to live a free life.*

The most precious thing, when you have a vocational child who is very connected to his intuition and has an elevated spirit, is not to tone it down trying to bring it to the "realm of what's really possible". Trust a great life will unfold for him or her.

Chapter 9 – Liam: Understanding Speed of Work, Speed of Results and Vocabulary

Liam was always in a hurry. He was at least five minutes early for his sessions and began to fidget about ten minutes before they were over. He was an architect by education but he became a project manager in a construction firm after graduating, and he had been working in Construction for over twenty years. In the beginning, the projects he managed were interesting and challenging: shopping malls, offices, residential buildings. More and more, as the years went by, he began to grow restless and it seemed that what once were interesting projects, didn't bring him any joy or excitement anymore. In our sessions, he enjoyed talking about art, architecture, philosophy. I didn't *find* the world of construction present in his vocabulary at all. He was planning to *retire* from the construction world and do something else, but he wasn't sure that it would be architecture (in which he had no real expertise other than his studies and his passion for it) or another profession.

He was a practical man. When he looked at his Abilities, he confirmed that his top natural ability was manual dexterity. He had an incredible need to use his hands during his work. For him, what led him close to discovering his calling in his mature years were these two concepts: *Speed of Work and Vocabulary*.

The *Speed of Work* can significantly influence your choice of profession. This variable alone can easily determine whether you are able to stay in a job or quit.

Liam, every profession happens at a different speed, it has a rhythm of its own. Let me explain what I mean by that, I said to him.

Imagine a hair stylist starting her day at 8 am, cutting clients' hair, blow drying, coloring, styling, on and on until 6 pm. Perhaps she gets to sit down for half an hour throughout the entire day. The pace is fast, with a lot of pressure on the physical body to sustain the work.

Such a fast work pace, especially when the body is involved, usually leads to fast results, so the stylist doesn't have to wait a week or two or ten or even a year for the result of her work to arrive.

The result comes in about 30-to-90 minutes once she starts working with a client. So the pace of her work is fast, and the results she gets are also speedy.

Some people are highly motivated by getting and seeing results each day, even several times a day, as is the case of many professions or activities: hair stylists, nail specialists, race car drivers, video gamers, cooks. The work they do each day brings a super fast result which usually happens that same day, for example when you're baking a cake or driving a car in a race. Pilots, bus drivers, taxi drivers, stock exchange brokers, news reporters, surgeons, emergency doctors, dentists - they deliver results multiple times a day. Most of the work they do doesn't have leftovers to be picked up again tomorrow. People who choose these professions most likely have short-term patience and it would be hard for them to engage in a type of work where results would only come in after a month or a year. These are people who get motivated by achieving results often, and fast.

Other types of work have a pretty fast daily pace but bring in results once every few weeks or months. For example, in the arts: painting, sculpting, writing (but not for daily newspapers), in various types of coaching, business and legal consulting, different types of therapies, teaching high school or college kids, in construction and in sports.

The work you do every day builds up to deliver results that require you to be more patient.

In very slow-paced types of work such as scientific/medical research, in psychoanalysis, results may come once every two to five to even ten years – for example in the research field. Talk about being patient, thorough and taking it easy! Not too many people can stay motivated when results take so long to arrive.

Why is this so important to you? The objective you had when you began working with me was that you fully understood the right framework for your work life, a framework that will allow you to stay in this chosen new profession a long time, building expertise and serving people around you, while feeling fulfilled.

You have to ask yourself all the important questions related to the Speed of Work and Speed of Results, and we are going to go through them together. In just a few minutes, you will realize why certain projects, part-time jobs or even longer-term activities stressed you out and at some point you stopped enjoying doing them. It is not that you are a procrastinator. One or more variables of that type of work did not fit your framework, your operating system if you will. Either the pace was too fast or too slow for either your body, your mind or your emotions, or you didn't feel you could get results as often and as fast as you need to in order to feel motivated.

So, to find out the work pace that is right for you, we'll use three variables and go back to your body, mind and emotions.

Just off the top of your head, if I were to ask you now, would you say that you would prefer a faster pace of work?

I used to think I liked the speed of project management, he said. *I thought it was fast, but in reality, it took a while until I saw results. What stressed me was that, even though I did my part, I was co-ordinating so many people who worked at different speeds. Some needed to deliver results quickly, every day, while others delivered at a slower pace. After so many years, I realized that I enjoy it most when my work has, let's say, a medium speed, when I don't have to deliver something daily but I also don't need to wait a year for a result. But there's another factor; I don't truly enjoy working or co-ordinating a big team. It was always very stressful. I like it more when I can take on a project and run it by myself from beginning to the end.*

Something else has been happening lately. I was never good at drawing, but I find myself making little sketches of people whose faces I find interesting, and then I sculpt them out of clay. Can you believe that ever since I became more and more frustrated with my work, I created quite a collection of sculptures? I think at least twenty five, in the last six months alone.

Well, let's look deeper at the pace of work that sculpting has. Is its speed matching the needs of your body, mind and emotions?

I'll give you examples from each category. A fast pace of work for the body is one where you constantly move your body, or parts of your body, such as your hands. This happens if you're a hair stylist, a shoe maker, a blacksmith, a cook, an athlete, a tennis player, soccer player.

A fast pace for the mind is one where your mind is literally on fire the whole day: you may be a judge, an attorney, a teacher, a life or business coach, a stock broker. You think, think, think the whole day with almost no break to contemplate and with very little movement of the body during your work.

A fast pace for the emotions, I would say, is when you are a priest, a trauma-specialized psychiatrist or therapist, a customer care specialist dealing with many unhappy clients every day, a divorce attorney or mediator, a couple's therapist. You have to filter so many emotions every day from so many people!

So, if you think you prefer a fast-paced type of work, would you prefer it to be fast-paced for the mind, for the body or for the emotions?

An example of a vocation that is fast-paced for body, mind and emotions is to be an ER doctor. Not too many people can sustain a super fast pace in all three dimensions every day.

Liam pondered on what I had just said. *I think I prefer a fast pace of work for my body, where I use my hands a lot throughout the day, but a medium pace for my thoughts and for my emotions. My mind was over stimulated throughout the past two decades, always thinking, never stopping to connect, just processing data all day. That is definitely not the right long-term recipe for me now.*

I love how this concept reveals a part of your vocational matrix, Liam. What about Speed of Results? Would you be more motivated if you'd see your work come to fruition daily, weekly, monthly, or could you wait longer?

In the construction world, he said, *a big project would come together in about two to three years. That is too long of a wait for me…I prefer the art world, where my work takes weeks or perhaps a whole month from concept to its final version.*

I'm glad you clarified that, I said. There is another concept that I believe will bring some insights. I'm talking about your work's **Vocabulary.** *If you were a college student or you were getting close to finishing high school, I would have placed great emphasis on this part of the discovery process. When you choose your vocation, you accept the fact that it will transform you little by little, it will influence what you talk about, the nature of your interests, how you see the world, and even your habits and vocabulary.*

With you, it became clear that the vocabulary of the construction world was not your favorite to use in conversation. You haven't talked about the field, its innovations, its challenges, at all. Instead, you talked a lot about art and architecture.

With younger clients, for this session, I always have a little fun with various vocabulary samples of different professions, such as accountant, lawyer, urologist, neurologist, dentist, architect, hair stylist, social media specialist, web designer and college math professor. Take a look at some conversations that take place in certain fields and imagine yourself talking about those things every single day, day after day, year after year. In your mind's eye, do you see yourself doing so with a straight face?

I gave him a workbook with several examples of conversations from many professions.

Take a look at this one, from the fitness world:

- *Alright, listen up, champ! Today's workout is gonna be a total game-changer. We're gonna kick things off with a dynamic warm-up to fire up those muscles and get your heart pumping. Think high knees, butt kicks, and some killer lunges to activate those glutes.*

- *Next up, let's hit the mat for some killer core work. We're talking planks, Russian twists, and bicycle crunches to sculpt that six-pack. Engage that core like your life depends on it, and feel the burn with every rep.*

What about the way a college math professor talks during his work?

- *Let us delve into the depths of vector calculus, where vectors roam freely in multi-dimensional spaces, guided by the principles of divergence and curl. Visualize the flow of fields, the flux through surfaces, and the gradients of potential, as we navigate the intricate web of mathematical abstraction.*

I can see where this is going, Liam said, closing the workbook. *The vocabulary of the construction world is not pretty. It's pretty vulgar. I like the practicality and the masculinity of the world itself, but the vocabulary doesn't represent who I am.*

Then you get the point that the profession that could be your vocation has a world of its own and you'd better feel a connection and a natural inclination towards its vocabulary, too.

Words do become actions, after all, and actions become habits. Can I ask you something? When you began studying Architecture, how did you like the classes?

I liked most of the classes, he said, *but I preferred the ones that had more to do with Art, Design or Photography.*

One other thing I like to do in my one-to-one work with future students is to have them take a look at the first year curriculum of the colleges they have in mind. See what the subjects you'll be studying are and also take a look at a syllabus and Bibliography, because if that will be your choice (let's say you choose architecture) your mind will absorb those words like a sponge and they will impact your being and your life more than any other interaction you'll ever have.

The work you'll end up doing long-term becomes a world of words, thoughts, behaviors, things you constantly care and talk about, filters through which you view reality. The energy of the words you use in your private life and that of the words you use at work are mixing all the time. The words at work can improve your relationship, elevate it, give it interesting topics of conversation that you also enjoy. How many people come home after a day's work and say to their spouse: *I don't want to talk about work at all, let's do anything else than that.*

Words, spoken, written and even just *thought*, create worlds and realities. Some are frustrating and confusing, aggressive and negative, competitive and stressful. Some are places of balance and clarity, where words are purposefully spoken to enhance the quality of relationships, both at work and in your personal life.

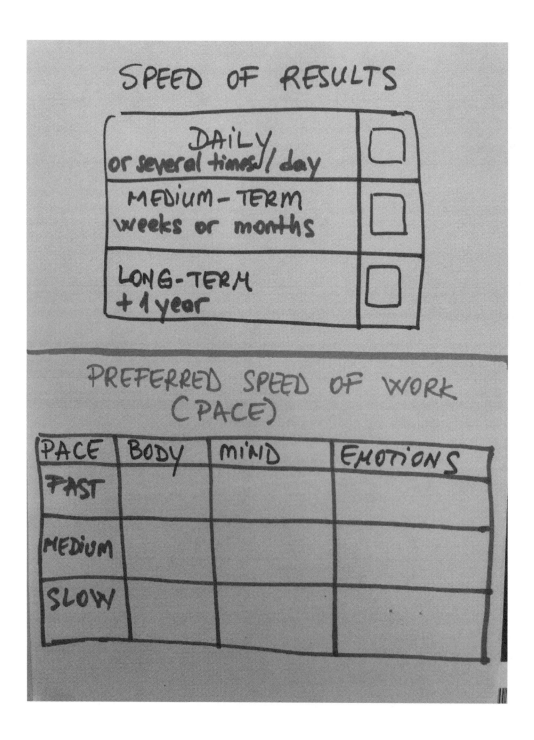

Chapter 10 – Francesca: Putting your Vocational Framework together

The purpose of the Vocational Triangle is to work like a personal matrix that will indicate if a certain profession meets the conditions to be a vocation for you. Let's say your conundrum was whether to leave the corporate world and become an entrepreneur in the wine industry. You did the discovery work and gathered or, better said, extracted important information about yourself. You synthesized it, categorized it and it became actionable because you understand it so well now. You understand yourself better.

The Triangle has three main variables that you did intensive discovery work on: Abilities, Lifestyle and People Around you. These three variables are the most important things when it comes to testing if a certain career is the right one for you. However, other factors such as the Speed of Work, the concept of Direct Utility, Vocabulary, have a great impact on the Lifestyle you will have once you practice that vocation.

The entire Triangle operates under the 70% Rule. As long as your choice of profession allows you to use and grow at least 70% of your key abilities on a daily basis, it matches your beneficial Lifestyle at least to an estimated 70% of how you imagine it, and allows you to spend at least 70% of your work time around the People that are right for you, you will stay in that profession long-term. A lower percentage for any of the three variables becomes a predictive factor that can indicate and almost guarantee you will want to change jobs.

Francesca was holding the large collage paper where she was supposed to synthesize the details of the work she did along our sessions.

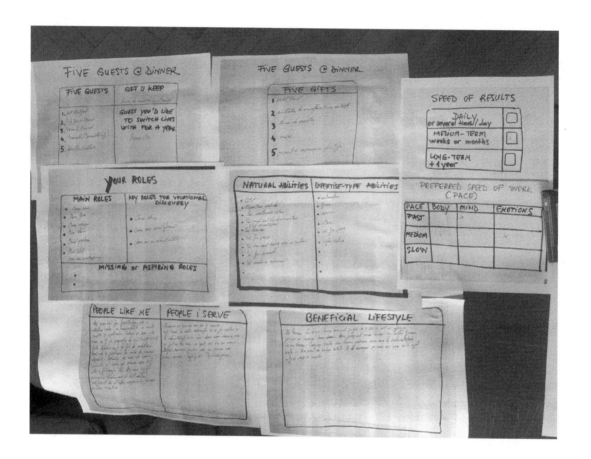

In her case, the discovery process was the most impacted by the realizations she had about Lifestyle. The Lifestyle she currently had would not allow her to take her mission-driven entrepreneurial venture to the level she was capable of attaining. Her long, brown hair surprised me from our first session; it reached beyond her waist and she seemed the most feminine and delicate woman I had ever seen. The words she was speaking seemed to create an entirely different impression of her: an Iron Lady who preferred numbers to people. She was in her early 30s, had studied engineering and then did a Master's in Business Management. She worked for a consulting firm until about a year ago when she quit and founded a start up with a great idea. The idea was an online beauty service, an app that would profile women's most suitable color palettes for make-up, as well as help them choose the right products. It took a little while to discover that her mind had been accumulating information and experience based on her parents' preferences for a safe career. But her top natural abilities were a mix of creativity, understanding numbers and an aesthetic eye.

So, Francesca, I said, on the left side of the Framework, you will synthesize all the information other than the Vocational Triangle.

You will start by filling in the names of your Five Guests at Dinner. Then, write in the Gift you chose to keep out of the five you received. Remember, I took four of them? Right under that, fill in the name of the Guest you most wanted to switch lives with for a year. That certainly is someone you aspire to! Right there you have a hint about the qualities of one of your aspirational roles, perhaps one you didn't initially write down when you identified your main roles.

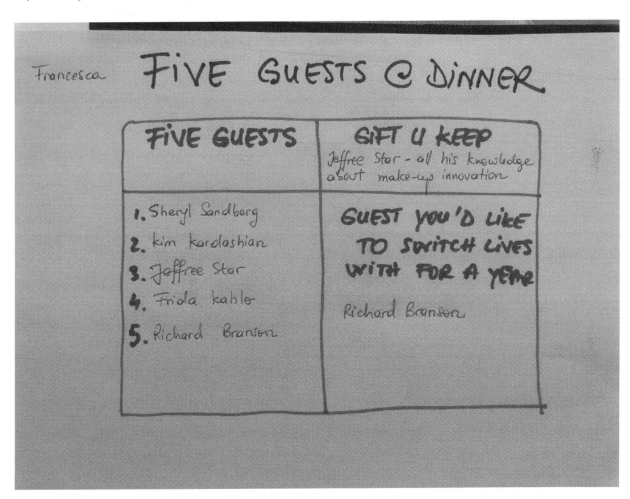

And speaking of Roles, they are the ones you'll be capturing next. Write them down, perhaps in the order your find most important. If you discovered a missing role that could be your aspirational and/or your vocational role, write that in the separate box. If you identified it right away, list it together with your other roles.

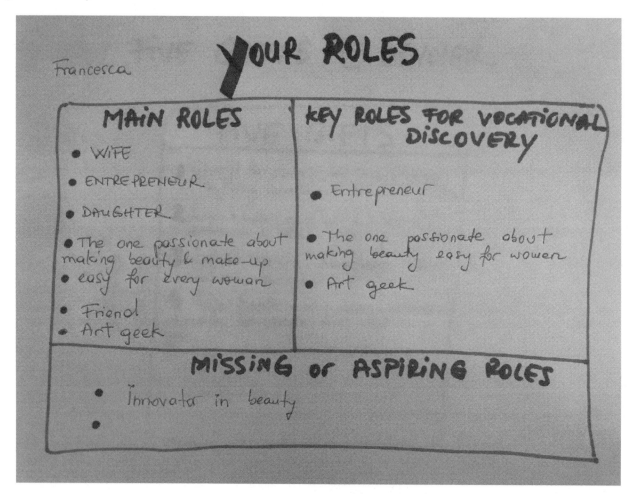

Next comes capturing the details of your preferred Speed of Work and how it relates to your body, mind and emotions. What kind of work pace do you feel would be good for you, and sustainable long-term? There is this table that gives you all the options. Take each variable and choose the right speed of work for it. Would you mind prefer to be constantly engaged while the body has a slower pace? Could your emotions deal with a big charge every day or perhaps you prefer to have the body moving most of the time as you work?

The Speed of Results motivates your mind to keep going. How fast should you get results in your work to stay motivated? Daily? Monthly? Long-term? Jot down that preference, which is a preference of the mind.

Francesca

SPEED OF RESULTS

DAILY or several times/day	☐
MEDIUM-TERM weeks or months	☐
LONG-TERM + 1 year	☑

PREFERRED SPEED OF WORK (PACE)

PACE	BODY	MIND	EMOTIONS
FAST		X	
MEDIUM	X		
SLOW			X

Lastly, on this particular page, write in the three Symbols or Objects you chose in the Treasure Chest Visualization. You can also write in their meaning and perhaps add more thoughts and insights you received about them yourself.

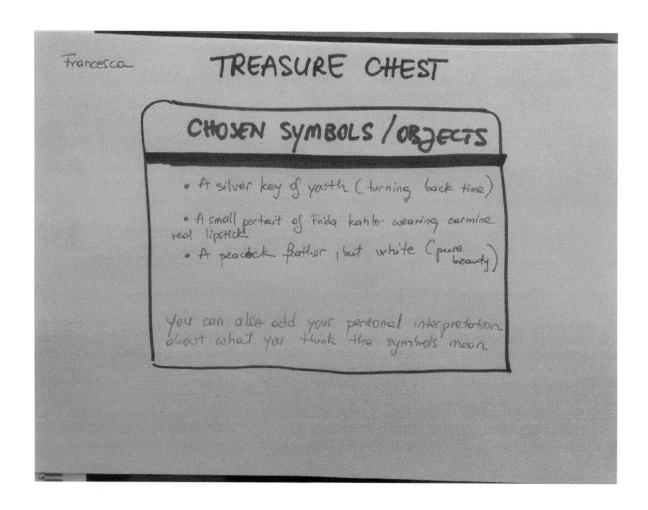

Now let's move to the Vocational Triangle itself and let's fill that in it so it becomes your personal Matrix.

On top of the Triangle you'll see two different boxes, to capture your Natural and your Expertise-type of abilities. Make sure to include the Expanded Natural Abilities in your List.

Francesca

NATURAL ABILITIES	EXPERTISE-TYPE ABILITIES
• innovation in color, imagining new color shades • seeing how make-up can harmonize features • to recognize architecture styles • to make great outfits for any body type • to understand programming • to inspire women to believe beauty is easy, and for everyone • to know and LOVE numbers • to create great products for women (ever since I was 15)	• C, Pascal, Fortran languages • building an online business • proficient English, Spanish • managing +10 people teams • managing +300,000$ budgets • project management • market research • •

Then, we'll move on to Lifestyle where you'll be writing in all the key points you captured in your Expanded Beneficial Lifestyle.

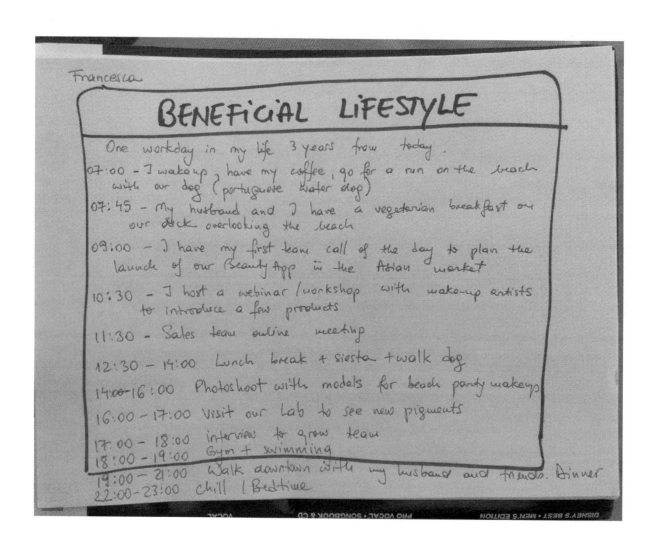

Lastly and, I would say, most importantly, you'll be describing the two categories of People most connected to your vocation: the people you work with and the people you serve.

> Francesca
>
> | PEOPLE LIKE ME | PEOPLE I SERVE |
> |---|---|
> | My colleagues are all young, 23-35, 50% women, 50% men, a team of 20 people. 12-13 are the same nationality, the rest are from all over the world. We meet online and share a passion for beauty, innovation in color, youthfulness, online markets. 5-6 have programming skills, 5 are great at online sales, 5 are make-up artists, 1 painter | I serve women all over the world who just want to find the PERFECT make-up style for them. No matter the nationality, skin color OR AGE, each woman using our APP will know which style, colors, products suits them best and give them a youthful, natural look, embracing nature's colors. |

It took about 30 minutes and Francesca diligently went through all the notes she had taken so far and filled in her Vocational Framework by hand.

Great, I said. Why don't you take a good look at it? Take a moment to let it sink in. You've already thought about all this…But here it all comes beautifully together.

*It's so clear to me, she said after a big sigh escaped her chest. The Beneficial Lifestyle that would allow me to take my work to the next level is not here, in this country. I am tied to family responsibilities and their expectations. My husband still works at the consulting firm where I have been previously employed. We had the same position in management and now he has been promoted to Deputy CEO. He likes his job, but it is not vocational. My entire family resents the risks that come with entrepreneurship but the people who are now thinking of investing in my app are at a whole different level of mind. They live in another world, in California. They think the idea could make millions in about a year, but I would have to hire a few people, spend more time in the U.S., travel so much more. The first two-three years may take me away from my family. I am really torn, because this idea is in fact **an expression of who I am**. What motivates me and gives me courage is the amazing feedback I have been receiving while testing he beauty app, from women in many different countries. The app is useful, easy to use, and they can implement changes in their beauty routine right away, with results they can share within the community created around the App.*

Francesca, I said, the Framework is a great testing tool and it will always tell you the truth about any work opportunity that comes your way. Once you know the truth, it's hard to be confused by other kinds of opportunities.

But it is also supposed to give you the power to stand up for your right to decide how to spend your work life, 1/3 of your entire lifetime.

If this idea is vocation-born, it is very important that you integrate it with your family members. I would say it is much more important to have your spouse on board than any other family member. Sometimes, choices we make are hard to communicate, especially when they are not something that the people around you, like your family, friends or colleagues expect. Perhaps, to some of them, a choice is not logical, it is not reasonable, it is not "realistic".

But courage to be yourself is always rewarded and one of the things that happens when you follow your vocational path is that the people like you will stay around you or will be drawn to you, whereas the people with different values and a different vision on life will want to distance themselves or will try to dissuade you.

I, too, attended several personal development programs. Some of them are so intense that they leave you with a strong desire to make an immediate change in your life. Sometimes, after an intense weekend of self-discovery, people quit their jobs or separate from their partner or make other choices. The choices seem brave and the sudden shifts create many ripples and many waves, like an earthquake, that people get to experience for a long time after that sudden change.

A sudden divorce has many consequences. To suddenly quit your job also has many consequences, and you did well to take your time and develop your project as well as find an initial investment before you left your employer.

My own spiritual practice taught me to be less impulsive. I used to make many impulsive decisions and, even though a high level of creativity can cause a high degree of spontaneity and highly sensitive emotions that tend to take control over our decisions, I, in all honesty, advise you to go about your vocational path in a balanced way.

That is going to save you so much time in the future! Remember, the choice of your vocation is your right. You do not owe your parents or your spouse or your mentor a duty of spending your life in a profession they may prefer. So there is no need to compensate them in any way because now your vocation is clear and you know communicating it to them may create conflict.

However, it is different when it comes to managing or harmonizing your Beneficial Lifestyle so that it doesn't lead to divorce or separation from someone you truly love.

Sometimes, though, if you're an adult who already has a steady job and family responsibilities, even if you may now be bursting with enthusiasm about having discovered your vocation or even perhaps having received confirmation of what your heart was telling you to do for a long time, I advise you to be patient a little while longer. When you have a family and responsibilities, they also have to be on board with your choice. If you love your partner and they love you, they will want to see and understand this process of discovery you went through.

I can give you the example of a young couple in their early thirties. He was a computer engineer who came to me because he felt he was ready to begin his entrepreneurial journey and open a small vegan restaurant together with his brother. We went pretty far and he came very close to scheduling a certain date when he was going to quit his job. But such an important choice must be one your partner in on board with, and even though his wife was supportive and she was practicing her vocation, she had a dream about their personal life. She wanted to have a baby in the next year or so. That was pretty much his timeline for opening the restaurant with his brother. She worried that the stress and financial investment of a new business may put too much pressure on them as a family right at the time when they baby would arrive. As a family, they made a plan about the sequence of the changes in their life. First, the baby arrived, a healthy baby boy. About six months afterwards, her husband was able to change his employment terms to work part-time for a year on a special project, and also work remote most of the time. His brother opened the small restaurant and today, four years later since he came to me for clarification, the two of them work at the restaurant full-time.

A clear vision of your work is inspiring and it is very likely that the person who loves you, your partner, will support your dreams and the changes you need to make.

For some of us, it is hard to communicate what we want to do to our closest relatives, especially if it is a big professional or personal change.

In highly vocational couples where there is a pretty sudden change in Lifestyle due to one's change of work, the other partner should be fully aware of the changes happening, of how these changes can impact their personal life, and have a plan to integrate those changes as a family. Sometimes entrepreneurs hit it big time and their family's life changes profoundly. It is not financial wealth that keeps them together, but their desire to share a mission that is bigger than one of them, and even to grow their children in a more socially-aware family.

You belong to a Group of workers

Like Tinkerbell belongs to the group of tinkers, you, too, belong to a group of vocational workers.

Every young man and woman, in every country, belongs to a group of people with similar abilities, who, together, can make a difference in various aspects of humanity's life.

Finding your vocation *will* put you in the right group. Many, many people mistaken their *hobby group* for their true group of similar-ability workers. Examples? There are plenty.

Many people leave their corporate jobs after years of working on different hobbies during the week-ends: painting, planting trees, dancing, making various crafts, cooking. Yet, when they are confronted with the *reality* of living their Monday-to-Friday life in the context and Lifestyle of a full-time painter, dancer, cook, they start doubting that that is their *final* vocational destination. So the search continues.

Your Group of workers is **not** defined by race, nation or religion. It is defined by abilities and the *people you serve, as a group, together, through those abilities.*

Where will you find this Group? It is not an organization per se. But the Group naturally forms around a cause. And you have to be careful to which kinds of causes/purposes/missions you adhere. Are those causes helping humankind evolve? Are they helping people be kinder, more generous, more brotherly? What virtues is the work of your group developing in people?

Think of organizations that produce and sell tobacco, alcohol, or other substances that, if abused, can cause serious disease in people's bodies and relationships. Do you want to be a part of a group of people that does that type of work?

Also, does the work of your group create differences and cleavages among people, rather than unify them?

These are very important questions. And something else to ponder upon:

Choose a vocation and a group that think progressively. Be a blacksmith, but integrate technology into your work. The world is not moving backwards. We cannot work against the complementarity that technology brings to our *mode of life. It is useless.*

Many fields will be reformed in the years to come, because young people will have integrated technology into their lives naturally, unlike my generation. Politics, religion, education, economy, will all be reformed and only young people, by having found their natural abilities and their right group, will be able to ride the wave of these reforms without resisting them for the sake of preserving the old behaviors.

Far from me the belief that today's young will become disengaged citizens, relying on technology to resolve their problems or to cater to their needs. I believe in an unprecedented escalation of people's mental and emotional capabilities, to the extent where creativity will bring so much advancement in science, technology, but also in our behaviors and relationships.

I also believe that high school should offer vocational discovery to all teenagers and that it is already possible to identify your group at the age of sixteen.

Of all countries, Switzerland remains the greatest example of how the vocational education system could work. "Compulsory education (kindergarten, primary and lower secondary) lasts eleven years in Switzerland. After that, the path typically leads to general education or vocational education and training. In many cantons, there's a big choice to be made after lower secondary school, around the age of fourteen or fifteen. Around two-thirds of young people opt for vocational training. This sees teenagers training on the job while also attending one-to-two days of vocational school a week. It's a system which has a good reputation internationally – it's been called the gold standard of vocational training.[2]"

---

[2] www.swissinfo.ch, The Swiss Educational System explained. See Link: https://www.swissinfo.ch/eng/sci-tech/the-swiss-education-system-explained/48148948

Work-life balance: an important factor to consider in the lives of vocational women and men

Far from me the antiquated idea that only men are made for tougher lines of work, be it intellectually or physically. Women have made so much progress in the past century, when it comes to having access to and achieving performance in most careers that men have worked in for much, much longer.

From an anthropological standpoint, men still want their line of work to bring them prestige, recognition and social acknowledgement of their worth. It's not necessary anymore for men to hunt and show their worth through the amount of prey they kill. But men do show their worth through their work, still. Whom do they show this worth to? Mainly women, yes, because a man's work makes him a high value partner or an unstable partner. Women, even though they are now employed and have successful careers of their own, still highly value the level of success a man has in his work. This does not only relate to financial gain. There is an important component that makes a man truly attractive as a long-term partner, and I would call that the "expert" factor. Women are more attracted to partners who are experts at something and feel they are more trustworthy and have a higher capacity to provide for a family, long-term.

Perhaps those of you who ponder on gender equality will argue that women-experts are also totally capable to be providers. However, it seems that, for women, it is still more important that their work life and family life are balanced and this *balance* is what makes high value women be more attractive to men who are looking for a long-term relationship. The vocational woman who puts 90% of her time in her work, regardless of how demanding that line of work is (E.R. doctor, lawyer, law enforcement), continues to have trouble to sustain a happy, long-term relationship.

An additional layer of understanding the connection between finding your vocation and also finding the right long-term partner, has to include these two distinctions:

Men who are experts at their work are seen as more trustworthy, are admired more and chosen as life-long partners, *even though* the time constraints of their line of work are higher than their life partner's. A man with a more flexible work schedule but with a lack of expertise (which translates in lack of economic success, too) in a certain field, will not be so attractive to a vocational woman.

Women, and especially those who have a vocational profession where they feel they can express their natural abilities on a daily basis, while also achieving expertise, are more likely to stay long-term in professions that will allow them to *balance* work and family life.

Work-life balance remains a component of family life that still mostly rests upon the shoulders of women/mothers, vocational as they may be.

Epilogue – A plea for parents and children

I'm ending this book with a special plea to the parents of teenagers who are hopefully reading it. I know you overcame many challenges and sometimes you came at your wit's end with your teen. You *just* want them to be ok, safe. Parenting teenagers, in our generation, has so many challenges and our time to parent is scarce. I know what I'm saying; my husband and I raise six children, out of which three are teenagers and one is a two-year old.

You worry that they spend too much time online. If they are boys, they play video games all day long. You wish you were around more and kicked them out of the house to play some sports or see some friends. If they are girls, you worry that social media is creating false life narratives and they won't know what is really valuable anymore, besides external beauty.

But *these are the times in which these children will be living their youth.* Their youth and adulthood will be lived in an era of integrated technology, where mental health will be the most precious aspect of the quality of life, not amount of assets.

Finding one's vocation is very important when it comes to maintaining a healthy sense of self-respect and self-admiration. My father used to tell me: it's better to be the best sanitation worker in the neighborhood than a mediocre attorney.

Your children cannot and will not *perform* or become experts in fields for which they don't have natural abilities. **Expertise is the result of working in a field long-term, but only when combined with enthusiasm does it produce performance.**

For those of you who are more pragmatic and authoritative, I hope this book opens your heart enough to trust that your child will be ok **when** he or she is the one making the choice for the type of work they will do. You have no idea how many young adults say these words: "now that I graduated from this or that college for my parents' sake, I can finally go study what I like."

I'm sure it is not only financial security that you wish your child to have in his or her adult life. If it is fulfillment, joy, self-love, self-respect, inner balance, mental health, that you *also* wish your child to enjoy as an adult, you *must let them discover their vocation, not tell them what it should or shouldn't be.*

FILL IN YOUR VOCATIONAL MATRIX AND ANALYZE YOUR OPTIONS

Use the templates in the book to fill in your own vocational matrix. Alternatively, write in a notebook after you are done reading each chapter and then put everything together, like Francesca did in the last chapter of the book.

You may have some options in mind when it comes to college choices or a potential next job. With the matrix by your side, look at your option (let's say it's law school or medical school or engineering school) and confront it against all the details you captured in your Vocational Framework. Does the lifestyle of that profession match your beneficial lifestyle? Do the people who work in that profession match the People you described in the exercise called People Like Me? Your list of Five Guests is indicative for the types of people and talents you like and admire the most. Are those people or their talents present in the area of work you are thinking of joining?

If you made a short list of two or three possible college options or potential jobs, one final step I always recomment you take, before making your decision, is to meet at least one person who has been successfully practicing each of the professions you are considering. Don't interview or meet people who dislike their work or their field of work; they will likely dissuade you from pursuing that path. Focus on those people who are happy with their choice. Ask the people you interview relevant questions about their daily lifestyle and what keeps their enthusiasm high despite challenges. Inquire about the main challenges in their work and the biggest rewards. Find out who are the people they love to serve. Ask how much money they make; it is important. Ask about how hard they work, too. More importantly, ask how they balance their work and their personal life, and if they feel they are continuing to grow their natural abilities even after five years in their profession.

Be as diligent and curios as you can; trust that, once you understood your vocational framework, the right opportunities will arrive, allowing you to use your abilities in the service of others.

Thank you for reading this book. I hope the time spent in this space brought you important insights and guided you towards your vocational path.

Made in the USA
Columbia, SC
24 September 2024